'THE ENEMY WITHIN'

By the same author:

The Story of Kinmel Park Military Training Camp
1914–1918

Welsh Soldiers, Civilians and Eisteddfodau in WWI

'The Enemy Within'

GERMAN POW'S AND ALIEN CIVILIANS IN NORTH WALES DURING WWI

Featuring the Dyffryn Aled German Officer POW Camp

Robert H. Griffiths

First published in 2017

© Robert H. Griffiths

© Carreg Gwalch 2017

ISBN: 978-1-84524-270-1

Cover design: Eleri Owen

Published by Gwasg Carreg Gwalch,
12 Iard yr Orsaf, Llanrwst, Wales LL26 0EH
tel: 01492 642031
fax: 01492 641502
email: books@carreg-gwalch.com
website: www.carreg-gwalch.com

DEDICATION

To my now well and truly grown up children, Claire (Anne) and Barry (Michael), whose father I am honoured to be, and of who I am immensely proud.

Claire lives in Bristol and travels the world on a regular basis, whilst Barry lives in Denbigh, North Wales, with his lovely wife Sarah and their adorable son Jackson, my absolutely wonderful grandson.

AND

To Ruth, my darling wife, my *cariad*, to whom I have been married thirty-nine years.

ABOUT THE AUTHOR

Robert H. Griffiths is a former police officer who now spends his time as a military historian, author and genealogist. He lives with his wife, Ruth, in Denbigh, North Wales.

Contents

Foreword

Following the success of his two previous books, Robert H. Griffiths has now turned his attention to the fate of the German and Austrian prisoners of war who were detained in North Wales during the First World War. Their stories interconnect with a remarkable range of themes and topics, each of which is of absorbing interest.

One of the notable features of the Great War is the importance of class and social status in the armed forces on both sides. Country houses such as Dyffryn Aled, near Llansannan, and Donington Hall, Leicestershire, were selected as appropriate detention centres for both Navy and Army officers. Dyffryn Aled's rural isolation made it especially suitable for such a purpose. The prisoners of war (and some internees) housed there belonged to a relatively privileged group, and the author has researched their backgrounds and military careers thoroughly.

The sources quoted by Robert H. Griffiths show how public resentment was evoked by the special treatment which enemy prisoners received. One can imagine how people in Denbigh or Abergele reacted as they saw prisoners of war travelling in carriages. After all, most local people coming to market in those days had to walk, and the British soldiers they might have seen training or on parade in the district would have been infantry, and on foot.

Inevitably, when a great European war broke out after a long era of peace, it was a profound culture-shock to a country like Britain, where traditionally the state had intervened as little as possible in people's lives. As early as the 1850s, during the Crimean War, commentators in Britain had questioned how a 'liberal state', with an elected government and minimal state regulation, would cope with fighting a major war against an autocracy like Russia, with its vast conscript armies and total state control. In the event, the major difficulty which Britain came to experience was the poor level of medical services and care available to its troops. It was the power of a free press and the determination of women volunteers like Florence Nightingale, Elizabeth Davies and Mary Seacole (three out of the 84 nurses who cared for some 10,000 sick and wounded men during the winter of 1854 to 1855) which forced a reform of the Army Medical Services, showing that public concern could not be ignored, whether in war or peace. Later, during the South African War of 1899 to 1902, that same public concern would be felt when Army doctors found that many of their new, young recruits were in poor physical condition – the consequence of having grown up in dire poverty. This concern would make its way into social legislation, with results such as the provision of school meals by local education authorities from 1906, and the establishment of a school medical service in 1908.

By 1914, it was clear that a modern war against an evenly matched industrial power made an increase in state power and control at home inevitable. Four days after the First World War was declared, the 'Defence of the Realm Act', known as 'DORA', introduced sweeping government powers, including press censorship (although this broke during the crisis over the munitions shortage in 1915). Over the course of the war, the level of state intervention continued to increase, coming to include the 'National Registration Act' in 1915, military conscription in 1916, and the control of agriculture and food rationing from 1916 to 1918.

Direction of labour and of the industrial economy towards war supply was masterminded in 1915 by David Lloyd George, then Minister for Munitions. Starting with a single desk and a chair in Whitehall, he built up a leviathan of a department which would come to control most of Britain's heavy production industries by 1916. It was Lloyd George, too, who famously articulated the need to shift from voluntary military recruitment to conscription, in a speech which he delivered in Conwy in May 1916:

> *Compulsion simply means that a nation is organising itself in an orderly, consistent, resolute fashion for war... Compulsion simply means the will of the majority of people – the voluntary decision of the majority... You cannot run a war as you run a Sunday-school treat, where one man voluntarily brings the buns, another man supplies the tea and another brings the kettle...*

This is the background against which the increasingly heavy hand of the state was being flexed throughout 1914 to 1918. The demand for the registration of 'aliens' must have felt particularly acute due to Britain's tradition of freedom of movement and immigration, especially during Victorian times, when Britain had fostered international free trade. Political refugees had always found shelter, including Karl Marx from Germany, the Hungarian nationalist Louis Kossuth, the former French Emperor Napoleon III, and the Russian Bolshevik leader Vladimir Lenin.

In 1914, nobody knew exactly who was living in Britain. People's births, marriages and deaths had been registered since 1837, and the population had been counted by decennial Censuses since 1801, but this mass of information was not a practical tool, and the microdata gathered was confidential. The 'National Registration Act' of 1915 sought to remedy this deficiency, and a comprehensive National Register was created, from which the very first 'ID cards', issued to everyone, were derived. It also made possible the adoption of conscription over the following months.

Fuelled by the invasion of neutral Belgium and the grim stories told by the 250,000 or more Belgian refugees who came to Britain, some 4,500 of whom lived in Wales for the war's duration, public anger against German nationals escalated rapidly. The 'British Nationality and Status of Aliens Act' was passed on 7 August 1914. This registration of so-called 'aliens' – citizens of foreign countries living in Britain – made it possible for the government to allay public fears over 'enemy aliens' at large in the land. The situation of long-standing German and Austrian citizens living in Britain was made difficult, and the stories of some who lived in Wales are considered very thoughtfully in this book. One case, which has become quite famous, occurred at Aberyswyth in October 1914. Dr Hermann Ethé was Professor of Oriental Languages at the University College of Wales, Aberystwyth. He had been born in Germany, of French descent, in 1844, and had taken his Doctorate at the University of Leipzig, teaching at Oxford University for three years before joining the professorial staff at Aberystwyth in 1875 – only three years after the University College opened its doors. He married an Englishwoman from Clifton, Bristol, in 1899. Dr Ethé had never applied for naturalisation, and the couple used to visit Germany regularly, on holiday. They were in Munich when war broke out in August 1914, and were at risk of being detained there. Nevertheless, they managed to travel north to Dresden, where the American Consul succeeded in getting them out of Germany and into neutral Holland.

Meanwhile, in Aberystwyth, Principal Thomas Roberts, of the University College, had applied to the Home Office to allow the Ethés to return to Britain, and they arrived in Aberystwyth by train on 13 October. The principal went to the railway station to meet them, and to warn them of the wave of anti-German feeling already sweeping the town.

The following day, two prominent local businessmen called a public meeting to demand that Dr Ethé leave the town. After the meeting, a crowd of some 2,000 people marched to the Ethé household on Caradoc Road and demanded to see the Professor. Only Mrs Harriet Ethé was at home, and she argued courageously with a hostile mob led by solicitor Enoch Davies, until two members of the University College's staff intervened. The mob threatened to return in twenty-four hours if the Ethés had not left Aberystwyth, to 'tear the house down stone by stone'. Given the dangerous situation in the town, where other German nationals were also being threatened, the Ethés decided to go, leaving almost all their possessions. Hermann Ethé never returned, and he died in Clifton in 1917.

Many studies of the 'Germanophobia' which occurred throughout the First World War emphasise the impact of two particular incidents on public opinion, one being the 1914 invasion of Belgium, in breach of international treaty; and the other being the sinking of the Cunard passenger liner *Lusitania* off the coast of Ireland, on 7 May 1915, by the German U-Boat *U-20*, commanded by Walther Schweiger. This attack caused the loss of 1,195 lives: men, women and children. In the days which followed the sinking, violent anti-German riots broke out in Liverpool, the *Lusitania*'s homeport. Shops believed to belong to Germans were smashed and looted, and it took days for order to be restored. Rioting also occurred in London and as far afield as South Africa.

Two who survived the *Lusitania* tragedy, a father and his married daughter, were the South Wales industrialist and MP, D. A. Thomas (later Viscount Rhondda) and his daughter Margaret Haig Mackworth. They were separated as the ship sank, and each believed the other was dead until they were brought ashore and reunited at Queenstown.

Lord Rhondda went on to become Food Controller in Lloyd George's government and the 'supremo' for food rationing. His daughter, Margaret, had been a militant suffragette before the war, and she continued to campaign for women's rights throughout her life as a businesswoman and journalist, being known and respected as 'Lady Rhondda' after inheriting her father's peerage.

One of the important issues Robert H. Griffiths raises in this book is the observance of international conventions in regard to the conduct of war. His detailed analysis of the *'Baralong* Incident' shows how seriously these were taken. Since the 1840s, several International Peace Congresses have been held, and one of the principal architects of them was the Reverend Henry Richard, of Tregaron, a Liberal MP who came to be known as the 'Apostle of Peace'. A Congress at The Hague in 1899 drafted a set of conventions to be observed by nation-states, including one on the conduct of war. A number of countries adopted these officially. Britain had signed up to the convention on the conduct of war in 1900, along with most of the countries who would later participate in the Great War. In 1907, an updated version was agreed. The 1907 Hague Convention was the one in force during the First World War.

A key feature of the 1899 Hague Convention was the status and treatment of prisoners of war. The convention included 20 Articles of Regulations designed to protect from abuse those who were captured during warfare on land. These protections were included in the 1907 convention, and extended to cover prisoners taken during warfare at sea. Two separate conventions, the Geneva Conventions of 1864 and 1906, governed the treatment of the sick and wounded during and after battles, and were administered and overseen by the International Red Cross, founded in Geneva in 1863. The Geneva Conventions were incorporated into the two Hague Conventions and are still in force today. Regulations governing the treatment of prisoners of war were superseded by the Geneva Convention of 1929, which was in force during World War II, and which was updated again in 1949. Each update and revision has aimed to identify and close the loopholes for abuse which the twentieth century's bitter catalogue of wars exposed.

Behind these laboriously drafted frameworks of international law and practice are the human stories – the stories of ordinary and extraordinary people who found themselves in deeply bewildering and traumatic situations. Individuals and families are often caught up and tossed like corks on the storm-tides of history. Robert H. Griffiths has rescued many of their remarkable stories from oblivion, and our understanding of those tempestuous times is much the richer for his labours.

Bob Morris (Robert M. Morris)
Historian and Author

Introduction

The waging of the First World War was catastrophically expensive for Britain. It also threw up major logistical problems in relation to the military prisoners of war (POWs) and 'alien civilians' who were interned for its duration. There is a list from early 1918 that provides details of some 566 different places where such internment took place. These sites were spread over the entire country, including its islands, and they ranged in size from 'housing' a handful of men to thousands.

From the outset, officer POWs were generally kept in separate camps to non-commissioned officers (NCOs) and lower ranks. This was done partly to 'divide and conquer', in that it deprived 'ordinary military men' of leadership, and partly because it was the class-conscious thing to do. While enemy Navy, Army and Air Force officers were housed in stately homes and country mansions such as Donington Hall (accommodation 500) and Philberds House (accommodation 600), NCOs and low-ranked POWs were kept in large camps like Frith Hill (capacity 6,000) and the Poundbury Camp (capacity 4,500).

At the beginning of the First World War, many captured officers came from the upper echelons of German society, including Prussian nobility. Within one month of the war's outbreak, Dyffryn Aled (accommodation 100) in Llansannan, near Denbigh, North Wales, was utilised for them. The rather remote Welsh country mansion had seen better days, and a detachment of Royal Engineers was sent to prepare it, with an emphasis on encircling the site with a twelve-foot-high wall of barbed wire. Officially, the British military authorities referred to Dyffryn Aled as a 'detention barracks', but others – including the British press and the housed German officers – called it a 'prisoner of war' or 'internment' camp.

The site operated from late August 1914 until late December 1918, during which time it was home to some of the most dangerous and capable men who had fought against Britain. These consisted of German and Austrian armed forces officers, along with a few high-ranking civilians, including a spy! Also among them were a different breed of enemy, thought more dangerous than any other, 'submariners' captured from '*unterseeboots*' (in English: undersea boats), otherwise known as 'U-Boats'. These U-Boat commanders and officers were highly intelligent and resourceful men, the type to be unsatisfied at Dyffryn Aled, even if they were provided with decent conditions. Each day of their incarceration, it would have been in their psyche to escape back to the Fatherland to continue their service.

The equitable treatment of enemy officers and high-ranking civilian POWs proved to be a delicate and difficult issue for Britain. If POWs were treated too well, there would be protest from the home press, goading the war-weary population (themselves suffering deprivations) to react with a mixture of jealousy and anger. On the other hand, if POWs were treated badly, other repercussions might ensue, such as the mistreatment of British POWs by the enemy, or the energising of their press. Mistreating POWs can also damage relations with neutral countries, some of which might be waiting to choose a side. For example, in the early stages of the First World War, due to a certain 'anti-British' sentiment in the United States, the younger nation looked as though it might side with Germany and the Central Powers. Because of this, the 'middle way' proved to be the best option for Britain – to treat POWs firmly but fairly, and to ensure they were not pampered.

The internment of 'alien civilians' in Britain was carried

out on a large scale at the behest of a public whipped up by the press. Both men and women were placed under suspicion and regarded as the enemy within; and thousands of military-aged Austrian, German and Hungarian men were 'rounded up' into all-male internment camps. One such large-scale but temporary camp was set up on the site of an old industrial works in Queensferry, North East Wales. It housed many 'alien civilian' men from North West England, including Manchester and Liverpool. However, the largest permanent internment camp for civilian men was not on the British mainland, but on the Isle of Man, at Knockaloe Camp, Patrick. Originally, this 22-acre camp was to accommodate 5,000 internees, but by the end of the war, some 24,500 were held there.

Other 'alien civilian' victims of the First World War included the British-born wives and children of foreign husbands, who was most frequently a German-born man. This meant great hardship when such a husband, the 'breadwinner' of family life in those days, was interned miles away and unable to continue with his work. Many British-born citizens also became enveloped in the 'spy fever' that abounded in wartime Britain, as they became suspected of being spies or fifth columnists without a shred of evidence.

Robert H. Griffiths
Denbigh, Spring 2017

Chapter One

An Overview of Dyffryn Aled

It is believed that Tudor Aled (1465–1525), the noted Welsh bard and master of the *cynghanedd* (in English: harmony), lived at the original Dyffryn Aled mansion around the year 1490. A nobleman, his Dyffryn Aled mansion was built on the opposite side of the river to the later mansion.

Designed by the architect Joseph Turner (1729–1807) around 1777, this later Dyffryn Aled began as an imposing three-storey building situated in the Aled Valley, between the villages of Llansannan and Bryn-Rhyd-yr-Arian in North Wales, before being extended over the years. Its exterior was cased with stone brought from the quarries of Bath, and its interiors had been designed by John Woolfe. For decades, it

DYFFRYN ALED GERMAN OFFICERS P.O.W CAMP 1914–1918

Sketch of the Dyffryn Aled mansion

was owned by wealthy landowners related to the Yorke family of Erddig, near Wrexham. Eventually, these owners fell upon leaner times, and in the late 1890s the site was leased and used as a branch of the Manchester Royal Lunatic Asylum, being known officially as the 'Dyffryn Aled Private Lunatic Asylum'. Then, following the death of a female member of the Yorke family in 1911, it was sold to the wealthy Winifred, Countess of Dundonald (1859–1924), who also owned the even more impressive Gwrych Castle, as well as several other properties in England and Wales.

At the outbreak of the First World War, Countess Dundonald kindly put Dyffryn Aled at the full disposal of the British government and military. It was decided to use the site, due to its barely accessible location, as an internment camp for German officers and their servants. These servants were low-ranking military personnel, who in the British Army would have been called 'batmen'. In the early days, a small number of German civilians of high status also came to be interned there.

The mansion possessed certain 'features' that would aid its use as an internment camp, and not ones normally associated with such a property; many of its rooms had iron bars on their windows, a legacy of its life as a lunatic asylum. Nevertheless, some preparations and alterations were required to make Dyffryn Aled 'more suitable'. This work was carried out by a detachment of the Royal Engineers, who marched through the nearby town of Denbigh on 28 August 1914. They prepared the mansion and the parkland (grounds) as a secure compound, installing many temporary buildings and enclosing much of the location with twelve-foot-high barbed wire. After both world wars, some looking back on Dyffryn Aled would come to describe it as 'the Colditz of World War One'.

Before the First World War, the local newspapers had described Dyffryn Aled as a 'pleasant country house'. After its outbreak, they feverishly informed their readers that up to 1,000 German prisoners of war would eventually be interned there – a totally incorrect 'ball-park figure', as it was never envisaged by the military authorities that more than two hundred 'German internees' would arrive. The site was not large enough to accommodate more, but more importantly, Dyffryn Aled was to house some of the most dangerous German officers, as well as a few German civilians thought to be high status enough for the 'secure' location, far away from the coast, large towns, major roads, and railway stations.

Chapter Two

Dyffryn Aled as an Internment Camp

Three local newspapers were to take a great interest in the 'happenings' at Dyffryn Aled during the First World War. These were the *Denbighshire Free Press*, the *Abergele and Pensarn Visitor*, and the *North Wales Chronicle*. The Saturday, 5 September 1914 edition of the *Abergele and Pensarn Visitor* informed its readers of 'The Happenings at Dyffryn Aled'.

> *The first portion of the guard to look after the German prisoners has already arrived at Dyffryn Aled. The guard consisted of twenty-five members of 'D Class' soldiers of the Royal Welch Fusiliers. These soldiers have been conveyed through the town of Denbigh en-route to Dyffryn Aled in three large brakes. But when some two miles out from Denbigh, near the village of Henllan, a telegram had been handed to the Officer-in-Charge of the group. As a result, the group were commanded to alight from the three brakes and to make the remainder of the journey on foot.*

On the following day, the first batch of German officers and their servants were conveyed from the temporary POW camp at Queensferry, Flintshire. Their journey took them by train via Rhyl on the Vale of Clwyd Railway. They alighted at Denbigh Railway Station and were escorted under guard through the town. Local people were amazed to have their first sight of the 'Huns', as the British national newspapers liked to call them. They were walked (not marched) up Vale Street, along High Street, over the top of Denbigh town and into Lenten Pool. There, they proceeded

Denbigh Railway Station circa WWI

along Henllan Street and out into open countryside. Once they reached Henllan village, it was just a matter of following country roads to Dyffryn Aled.

The official address for Dyffryn Aled, as stamped upon all outgoing mail, at least from 1914 to 1916, was as follows:

DETENTION BARRACKS
OFFICERS PRISONERS OF WAR
DYFFRYN ALED
LLANSANNAN
ABERGELE
NORTH WALES

Despite the above, some correspondences to and from Dyffryn Aled referred to it as being 'near Denbigh, Denbighshire'. At the very least, the German POWs housed there had arrived through Denbigh, and they obtained many of their 'mess supplies' from its shops, while the town's 'lock-up' on Love Lane kept apprehended escapees overnight. By those interned at 'Dyffryn Aled Officer's Prison Camp', it was referred to in German as *'Dyffryn Aled Offiziersgefangenlager'*.

Lieutenant-Colonel R. C. Drury had been appointed as the first commandant (governor) of Dyffryn Aled. Some of the first prisoners of war to be placed in his charge were Imperial German Navy (in German: *Kaiserliche Marine*) officers captured after the naval battle near Heligoland Bight (in German: *Helgolander Bucht*) in the North Sea, which had taken place on 28 August 1914. The *Denbighshire Free Press* edition commented the following in their Saturday, 19 September 1914 edition:

DYFFRYN ALED CAMP

Prisoners of War continue to arrive at Denbigh en-route for Dyffryn Aled. Several lots have come this week. Most of the men have been arrested in this country and have not been in the fighting line. Strangely enough, the men are sent from all parts of the country, even from the North of Scotland. They are most carefully guarded and enclosed in twelve feet of un-climbable barbed wire fencing. When one sees the Scottish kilts and uniforms of the guard it brings to mind happier days when the Lancashire and Liverpool Scottish were in our midst.

Initially, a small number of senior German non-military officials were housed in Dyffryn Aled, but they were soon moved or exchanged for British officials who had found themselves 'trapped' in Germany at the outbreak of war. The newspapers were not yet fully aware that the German prisoners being sent to Dyffryn Aled were naval officers from German U-Boats, destroyers and other enemy vessels that had been sunk or captured in the North Sea and the

Scapa Flow. If one seeks evidence that Dyffryn Aled was indeed 'THE' internment camp for the most dangerous of the enemy, then it can be found in the records held in the National Archives. Nominal rolls from late 1915 and early 1916 reveal the following:

Donington Hall, German Officers POW Camp
From a total of 147, four were from U-Boats.

Holyport (Philberds House), German Officers POW Camp
From a total of 127, two were from U-Boats.

Dyffryn Aled, German Officers POW Camp
From a total of 51, twenty were from U-Boats.

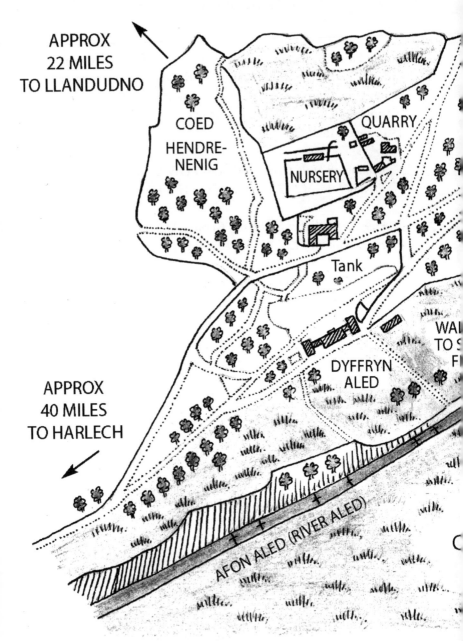

APPROX
22 MILES
TO LLANDUDNO

COED
HENDRE-
NENIG

QUARRY

NURSERY

Tank

WA[
TO S
F[

DYFFRYN
ALED

APPROX
40 MILES
TO HARLECH

AFON ALED (RIVER ALED)

DYFFRYN ALED GERMAN C

Plan of Dyffryn Aled

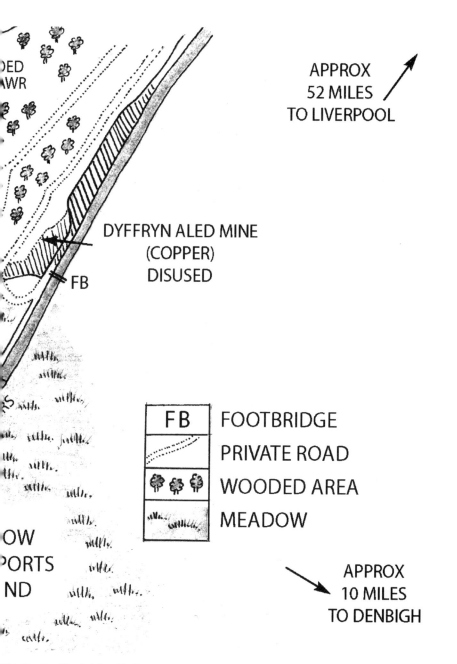

APPROX
52 MILES
TO LIVERPOOL

)ED
\WR

DYFFRYN ALED MINE
(COPPER)
DISUSED

FB

| FB | FOOTBRIDGE |
| PRIVATE ROAD |
| WOODED AREA |
| MEADOW |

OW
ORTS
ND

APPROX
10 MILES
TO DENBIGH

RS P.O.W. CAMP 1914-1918

Chapter Three

Wolfgang von Tirpitz

The *Birmingham Daily Post* of Monday, 31 August 1914 had this news to impart to its readers:

ADMIRAL TIRPITZ'S SON A PRISONER

Eighty German prisoners from the sunken cruiser Mainz were landed at Leith one evening from a British cruiser. There were eight officers, including a son of Admiral von Tirpitz, the German Naval Secretary, and seventy-two men, sixteen of whom were wounded. A special train was in waiting for the prisoners. The wounded were attended by a staff of nurses and ambulance men in a newly erected dressing station at Victoria Dock. They were afterwards conveyed in Red Cross motor-cars to Edinburgh Castle.

The Saturday, 19 September 1914 edition of the *Abergele and Pensarn Visitor* newspaper elucidated further:

Amongst the inmates of the German Prisoner of War Camp at Dyffryn Aled is young von Tirpitz, son of Admiral von Tirpitz, Chief of the German Navy. One of the German prisoners speaking to one of the guards at Dyffryn Aled in broken English said, 'We shan't be here long, the Emperor will soon relieve us.'

The *Liverpool Echo* of Friday, 8 January 1915 added:

YOUNG TIRPITZ'S REQUEST

The Germans celebrate the sinking by U-Boat of the S.S. Lusitania.
Grand Admiral Von Tirpitz depicted on this 1915 postcard

Young Tirpitz, son of Admiral von Tirpitz (Commander-in-Chief of the German Navy), made a request to his guardians at the Dyffryn Aled internment camp, Denbighshire, the other day, for a certain comfort. It was politely refused him, the official explaining 'that is being reserved for your Dad'.

The request from the young Wolfgang von Tirpitz had been for permission to occupy an apparently vacant room discovered inside Dyffryn Aled, so that he would no longer have to share a space with several fellow German officers. One can only guess that he was not too amused with the flippant reply he received. A few months later, following the sinking of the *RMS Lusitania*, the blame for which fell upon his father, Grand Admiral Alfred Peter Friedrich von Tirpitz, his request might have provoked a much stronger reaction.

Young von Tirpitz had been made a prisoner of war after the sinking of the *SMS Mainz*, a *Kolberg*-class light cruiser of the Imperial German Navy assigned to patrol around the island of Heligoland Bight. At about 8.00 a.m. on 28 August 1914, a superior force of British ships, including battle cruisers and light cruisers, had attacked a German torpedo boat out on patrol, leading to engagement with the fleet to which it belonged. One of the casualties of the battle which followed was the *SMS Mainz*, leaving many of its officers and crew swimming for their lives. Sub-Lieutenant (in German: *Oberleutnant zur See*) Wolfgang von Tirpitz, son of Grand Admiral (in German: *Grossadmiral*) Alfred von Tirpitz, the architect and head of Germany's High Seas Fleet, was picked up wearing his full officer's uniform. The young 'Wolf', as he was known by family, friends and fellow naval officers, was something of a catch for the British Royal Navy.

Winston Churchill, then the First Lord of the Admiralty, kindly informed Grand Admiral Alfred von Tirpitz, via the United States Embassy in Berlin, that his son was alive and in British hands. This was not something the family

SMS Mainz

members of most POWs on either side could expect, which demonstrates the influence of class throughout the First World War. The Grand Admiral was to show no appreciation for the gesture of kindness, and he is credited, somewhat unfairly, with the German U-Boat offensive that saw every allied ship as a legitimate target for sinking, as the *RMS Lusitania* and its passengers were to find out in May 1915!

Why did Winston Churchill act in such a benevolent manner to one of Britain's greatest foes? The answer is that Wolfgang von Tirpitz was on visiting terms with Mr and Mrs Churchill prior to the outbreak of war, and he had played tennis with Mrs Churchill at the Queen's Club. Such are the vagaries of war for the higher echelons of society. While 'ordinary soldiers' were shooting, bombing and hacking each other to pieces in the trenches, niceties were still being observed for those of the 'officer class', as if the two sides were taking part in some admirable sporting contest.

On 30 August 1914, Wolfgang von Tirpitz was interned at Redford Camp in Edinburgh, as were many other POWs from the Battle of Heligoland Bight. This site acted as a transit camp, housing POWs and 'alien' persons until they could be moved elsewhere. Wolfgang von Tirpitz's destination was, of course, Dyffryn Aled, which remained his home for over three years before he was moved again, this time to Kegworth Camp, and then later to Holland under a POW exchange deal.

During Wolfgang von Tirpitz's time at Dyffryn Aled, he was, due to his family connections, the subject of several newspapers articles. On 3 December 1914, the *Daily Mail* correspondent Frederic Wile visited the mansion. In mid-January of the following year, a number of newspapers published his account:

GERMAN OFFICERS IN THE PRISON CAMPS NARRATIVE OF THE GRAND ADMIRAL'S SON

To-day, through the courtesy of the War Office, I have had the opportunity of studying what the Germans call 'English barbarism' with my own eyes and ears. Permission was given me to penetrate the remote but picturesque wilds of Denbighshire, and pay a visit to 'Dyffryn Aled', the Welsh estate of Lady Dundonald, which is now doing duty as 'detention barracks', for enemy officers who fall into British hands as prisoners of war.

'Dyffryn Aled', which means Valley of the Aled, is a glorious country seat nine or ten miles distant from Denbigh, so secluded amid wooded hills, some 600 feet above the level of the sea, that it is accessible only by vehicle from the world without. At present Lady Dundonald's rambling old sandstone mansion of some twenty-five or thirty rooms shelters ninety-eight German officers and thirty-seven soldiers and civilians, also held as prisoners of war. The camp is in the charge of Colonel R. C. Drury, commandant.

Later on, in the course of this narrative I shall quote the evidence of 'Dyffryn Aled's' most distinguished inmate, Oberleutnant Wolf von Tirpitz, son of Grand-Admiral von Tirpitz, secretary of the Imperial German Navy. In confirmation of my own impressions that the prisoners who have the good fortune to be interned there are the recipients of treatment which is the last word in comfort, courtesy, and consideration. Every moment of my two hours at the camp I was wishing that I might have been accompanied by the editors of the 'Frankfurter Zeitung', the 'Cologne Gazette', the 'Hamburger Freindenblatt', and the 'Berliner Lokal-Anzeiger', who have been shrieking themselves red in the face over British 'inhumanity' to their captured compatriots.

My visit to 'Dyffryn Aled' happened to synchronise with

a call paid to the camp by a member of the American committee interested in the welfare of prisoners of war in the various warring countries. As this visitor had a special permit to converse with Oberleutnant von Tirpitz, it was my great pleasure to be present during an extended conversation with him. I was thus enabled to hear from his own lips not only his modest story of his thrilling and gallant experiences in the Battle of Heligoland Bight on August 28th, but his outspoken tributes to the knightliness with which he has been treated from the moment of his rescue by British sailors in the waters of the North Sea.

The Lieutenant was watch-officer in the light cruiser *Mainz*, and during the engagement he was 'spotting' in the crow's nest with a brother officer. Von Tirpitz is a handsome young German of twenty-seven, with conspicuously clean-cut features, greyish-blue eyes, wavy blonde hair, tall, trim and erect. Un-bearded like most German naval officers, whose ambition it used to be to ape every external aspect and mannerism of their British confreres, Oberleutnant von Tirpitz could easily enough, in the becoming new suit of light grey mufti which he wore to-day – made to measure in England since his arrival – be mistaken for an officer of Admiral Jellicoe's squadron. He speaks English with absolute fluency – thanks as he explains to the fact that both his mother and two sisters are 'Cheltenham College girls', and that he himself once spent three months in the home of a clergyman near Oxford. He has also crossed to the United States and is proud of his ability to employ the Amurrican accent. 'But I am glad to think I look like a good German after all', he smilingly observed in response to the suggestion that he might 'just as well be British or American'.

Oberleutnant von Tirpitz when asked whether he was aware that Mr Winston Churchill had promptly telegraphed to Grand-Admiral von Tirpitz advising him of his son's safety said, 'Yes, my parents wrote me about that in grateful terms. I know Mr and Mrs Churchill quite well. I played tennis with Mrs Churchill at the Queen's Club last summer and lunched with them both.'

Then he went on to say: 'My part in the Heligoland fight wasn't very important, I fear. Of course, it was my baptism of fire. My chief recollection of the engagement in general, is that we were very heavily outnumbered. I think I must have counted at least twenty-five British men-of-war from my place in the crow's nest of the Mainz before I was brought down.

'It is only by a miracle that I was spared. The officer on duty alongside me in the crow's nest was torn clean through the waist-line by shell-fire, while I remained untouched. The poor fellow was too far gone to swim as I did, after we were swept from our lofty perch and dashed into what seemed certain death in the sea. I think I stayed in the ship as long as it was humanly possible. I certainly had no other thought than to go down with her. I assuredly did not expect to come through the awful experience with my life. But, you see, I had not reckoned fully with the knightliness of our foe. I swam for about twenty minutes in full uniform, except for cap and sword, and with some half-burnt life-belts to help me, when I was picked up by one of the cutters of the cruiser Liverpool. Cutters from that and other ships were now busily scouring the sea in all directions, making the utmost efforts to save German sailors from drowning. All of us were treated exactly as if we were comrades, not enemies. I am quite sure Admiral Beatty's sailors made every possible effort to rescue our fellows. It was not the Britishers fault that more of us were not saved.

'British hospitality, which began that misty August afternoon – the fight was at its height about 2 p.m. – has been continued, so far as my comrades and I here at Dyffryn

Aled are concerned, to this very hour. I cannot say I am
exactly happy; I am a prisoner in the enemy's country. But I
am quite as comfortable and well cared for as any man in my
position has reason to expect – in fact, more so.

'You can judge from my appearance that I am absolutely
fit, as the English say. You have been round the camp and
know for yourself that everything is done for our comfort,
convenience, and happiness, which is compatible with our
surroundings. I am fond of the violin, and one of my first
purchases here was an instrument. How to pass the time, you
see, is our greatest hardship. I hadn't been in England long
before I began to get convincing evidence that though these
people are at war with us they remember that, as far as many
relationships in the two navies are concerned they are
fighting old friends. At Kiel, in the last week of June, we had
a fine English squadron visiting us. I was often on the
Southampton and the Birmingham – the latter was to help
sink us at Heligoland nine weeks later! – and I became well
acquainted with Vice-Admiral Sir George Warrender and
one of his flag-officers, Lieutenant Buxton, who offered to
send me money, clothes or anything else I needed. But my
allowance here is quite sufficient to take care of all my urgent
needs.'

Pages 373 to 374 of Max Hastings' book, *Catastrophe:
Europe Goes to War 1914*, enlighten us as to what Wolfgang
von Tirpitz's father, Grand Admiral Alfred von Tirpitz,
thought of the 28 August 1914 action in Heligoland Bight,
and the fate of his son:

… *Yet there were larger, physiological forces in play which
were and remain, underrated by critics of the Heligoland
Bight action. Its impact on the High Seas Fleet went far
beyond the trifling material losses. German sailors*

recognised that they had suffered a humiliation. British ships had steamed and skirmished with impunity within a few miles of the coast of the Fatherland. Hundreds of thousands of civilians ashore had heard the gunfire, and trembled. Admiral Tirpitz raged, not least because his son Wolfgang was a Lieutenant on the lost Mainz. He spoke in extravagant terms to Albert Hopman: 'We disgraced ourselves. I knew that I had to sacrifice my son. But this is dreadful. We came under fire, and in consequence saw the end of our fleet.'

Tirpitz refused to be comforted by Hopman's reminder that the British had recovered German survivors: his son might be among them. He persuaded himself the young officer must be dead. Yet, next day, the British sent word that they indeed held young Tirpitz as a prisoner.

In the House of Commons and the British press, claims were made that Wolfgang von Tirpitz had been immediately allowed to return to Germany, or that he was out of his internment and visiting friends. Though these stories were baseless, this did not prevent them from appearing. Here is an excerpt from the *Evening Telegraph* edition of Monday, 21 June 1915, which references such claims:

VON TIRPITZ'S SON NOT RELEASED ON PAROLE OR OTHERWISE

Statement in Commons To-day

In the House of Commons this afternoon Mr Tennant, Under-Secretary for War, in reply to Mr Ronald McNeill, said that Lieutenant von Tirpitz, prisoner of war, and son of the German Admiral, had not been released on parole or otherwise. The statement that Lieutenant von Tirpitz, son of the German Admiral responsible for the submarine policy, had been released on parole excited public indignation. It was with a view to stilling this feeling that the question was put in the Commons to-day.

Von Tirpitz was one of the prisoners rescued from the German cruiser Mainz, which was sunk in the Battle of Heligoland Bight on August 28th. He was interned with a number of others at Dyffryn Aled, a beautiful country seat near Denbigh, North Wales, where, as he himself acknowledged, everything compatible with their surroundings was done for their comfort, convenience and happiness.

The *Daily Mirror* edition of Monday, 14 January 1918 carried the information that Wolfgang von Tirpitz and other German officer prisoners who had been interned for a long period were sent to neutral Holland for a 'kinder' form of internment:

VON TIRPITZ GONE!
GERMAN PIRATE CHIEF'S SON AMONG
PRISONERS SENT TO HOLLAND.
EMDEN CAPTAIN'S SILENT MOOD

Amsterdam, Sunday – Three Dutch ships bringing German prisoners from England to Holland for internment, and wounded and civilians who are being sent home arrived at Rotterdam from Boston yesterday evening, after a stormy crossing. The presence on board of Captain von Mueller of Emden fame, Captain Wallis and Lieutenant von Tirpitz, son of the Grand Admiral evoked considerable interest. Dutch reporters vainly tried to get von Mueller to talk about his adventures, and he emphatically disavowed any intention of writing a book. Many of the infantry officers have been captured in South-West Africa. The Germans did not give the Dutch pressmen a very good account of their captivity, some even complaining of the food, but they acknowledged the good tone that marked British conduct towards the prisoners.

The Telegraaf says that the submarine captains, of whom there were five in the party, had declared they were exceedingly sorry when obliged to torpedo a ship, but war was war.

Prince Henry of the Netherlands subsequently inspected the ships and talked with several well-known German officers.

Wolfgang Rudolf Gustav von Tirpitz had been born in Kiel, Germany, on 21 April 1887, to Alfred Peter Friedrich von Tirpitz, then a corvette captain (in German: *korvettenkapitan*) in the Imperial German Navy, and Marie Auguste von Tirpitz (nee Lipke).

Throughout the 1890s, Alfred von Tirpitz had worked to transform the modest Imperial German Navy into a world-class naval force which could rival the maritime might of Britain. He did so by adopting much of what was great about the British Royal Navy, and for this, on 12 June 1900, an appreciative Emperor (in German: *Kaiser*) Wilhelm II elevated him to the Prussian nobility. Like his son, Alfred von Tirpitz spoke English fluently, and he even sent his two daughters to Cheltenham Ladies' College, the prestigious Gloucestershire boarding school for girls aged between eleven and eighteen.

After Wolfgang von Tirpitz's years of internment as a POW, he returned home in early 1919 to find a defeated and utterly demoralised Germany. He was promoted to captain-lieutenant (in German: *kapitanleutnant*) in July of that same year, with seniority and rank backdated to 13 January 1917. On 22 November 1919, he retired from what had been renamed the 'Provisional Imperial German Navy' (in German: *Vorlaufige Reichsmarine*) following the abdication of Emperor Wilhelm II, who had fled to the Netherlands in permanent exile.

Post-First World War, the defeated Germans had to dismantle a great amount of their military installations and hardware as 'punishment'. These included fortifications and harbours on Heligoland, the sparsely populated islands in German possession, located in the south-eastern corner of the North Sea. The Heligolanders were themselves causing some disorder, for they were frustrated with what they regarded to be Prussian (German) bureaucracy stifling their everyday lives. Wolfgang von Tirpitz, now a naval correspondent, was there to report to the German authorities with the latest happenings, but he was pointedly unhappy at what was taking place around him, the presence and supervision of British Royal Navy officers making it all the worse! *The Times* reported on this matter in their edition of Thursday, 18 August 1921:

It is evident that the Germans are paying close attention to the activities of the British naval officers controlling the work of the dismantlement of Heligoland, but it is not every writer who confesses to such extreme measures of espionage as Herr Wolfgang von Tirpitz, the naval correspondent of the German Gazette. After recounting the destruction done in the former submarine harbour as seen during a visit of 'inspection', Herr Wolfgang von Tirpitz describes the arrival of an English yacht, the crew of which he followed to the Empress of India Hotel, where the Naval Commission has its headquarters. He writes: 'From outside one looked into a brightly lighted room. The gold-striped naval officers of the Commission were sitting with their pipes in their mouths highly satisfied with life. There was breakfast with eggs, toast and marmalade, quantities of food for lunch, and 5 o'clock tea, just as in London, Cape Town, Singapore and Cairo. With a troubled heart, I returned to the Oberland.'

While continuing his walk, Herr Wolfgang von Tirpitz asks: 'Why were we treated like this? Why must the best that German labour produced in a generation be destroyed?' But he confesses that neither the sea, nor the skies, could give him an answer.

His peevish remarks, particularly those about the fayre being enjoyed by the British officers on Heligoland, are questionable when one considers the style in which Wolfgang von Tirpitz and his chums wined and dined as POWs at Dyffryn Aled.

In 1953, aged sixty-six, Wolfgang von Tirpitz visited Britain and went to see his old family acquaintance, Sir Winston Churchill, at his estate of Chartwell near Westerham, Kent. Wolfgang, as well as making a cordial visit, took the opportunity to ask of 'the great man' that three old, senior and prominent figures of Nazi Germany be released from Spandau Prison, where they had been sent following the Nuremberg Trials of the 'Top Twenty-Four Nazis'. Wolfgang von Tirpitz publicly stated that his only interest in the matter was to help these old gentlemen regain their freedom, since he was a former officer himself, and the three had acted well during their imprisonment. Sir Winston Churchill informed von Tirpitz that the decision of whether to release convicted Nazi war criminals was not up to Britain alone, but a decision for the four Allies, namely the United States, Russia, France and Britain. Churchill did, however, proffer that if the matter was up to Britain alone, then the three men would have already been released.

The first of the three men in question was Eric Raeder, who from 1928 until his retirement in 1943 had been the

Commander-in-Chief of the 'War Navy' (in German: *Kriegsmarine*), formerly known as the 'Navy of the Realm' (in German: *Reichsmarine*), and before that the 'Provisional Imperial German Navy'. Although sentenced to life imprisonment, he would be released on the grounds of ill-health on 26 September 1955, dying 6 November 1960. His successor as head of the War Navy was Karl Donitz (sometimes spelt Doenitz), the initiator of the U-Boat campaign, and the second prisoner who Wolfgang von Tirpitz sought freedom for. Donitz had been convicted at Nuremberg of ordering unrestricted submarine warfare. Found guilty, he received a sentence of ten-years imprisonment. He was released from prison on 1 October 1956, dying 24 December 1980 at Aumuhle in Schleswig-Holstein, Germany. The third of the three men was Baron (in German: *Freiherr*) Konstantin von Neurath, a high-ranking Nazi bureaucrat who served as the Nazi Minister of Foreign Affairs from 1932 to 1938, and the Protector of Bohemia and Moravia from 1939 to 1943. He fell out with Adolf Hitler in 1943 and resigned his position. Sentenced to fifteen-years imprisonment at Nuremberg, he was released from his imprisonment after suffering a heart attack on 6 November 1954, dying 14 August 1956.

Over the years, Wolfgang von Tirpitz proved extremely reluctant to speak with historians about his late father, Grand Admiral von Tirpitz, for he believed they wrongly represented his father as a warmonger, the evil force behind the German Emperor Wilhelm II's First World War. By the 1960s, the elderly Wolfgang von Tirpitz was living with his wife, Elizabeth von Tirpitz (nee Sering), in a modest cottage in Irschenhausen, Bavaria, Germany. He relented, allowing Professor Jonathan Steinberg to visit his home and have access to certain family manuscripts. During their conversations, as recorded in Corrado Pirzio-Biroli's book,

My Great-Grandfather Grand Admiral von Tirpitz – German Leader After Bismarck and Before Hitler, Wolfgang von Tirpitz told of something quite amazing which concerned himself and Hitler.

On 1 April 1939, Wolfgang and his sister Ilse attended the launch of the mighty German battleship the *Tirpitz.* It was Ilse, in fact, who was to christen the vessel named after their late father. Upon donning his naval uniform that morning, Wolfgang had been pleased to see it still fitted him after two decades. In his tunic, he concealed a dagger with which he intended to kill Hitler, who was also to be present at the launch of this great Nazi 'beast of a ship'. Sadly, in the moment Wolfgang reached to withdraw his dagger, he thought of his three young sons and hesitated.

Wolfgang von Tirpitz was no Nazi, and when interviewed during the latter years of his life, he would state with great force and bitterness:

'Anyone from my class who tells you that he did not know what was going on is lying.'

This is a very telling indictment on the many high-profile Nazis who after the war denied knowledge of, let alone involvement in, the atrocities of the vile regime.

Chapter Four

Captain Theodore Schlagintweit

The *Manchester Courier and Lancashire General Advertiser* of Saturday, 3 October 1914 contained the following:

> *Captain Schlagintweit, the ex-German Consul in Manchester, and the son of Admiral von Tirpitz are still at Dyffryn Aled. Captain Schlagintweit is often seen in Denbigh where he makes purchases on a large scale for his fellow prisoners. He is always in the charge of a British Officer. There is no truth in the reports that alleged plotters at Dyffryn Aled had been court-martialled and that Captain Schlagintweit was unwell.*

As was reported in the Monday, 24 August 1914 edition of the *Dundee Evening Telegraph*, Captain Theodore Schlagintweit, the German Consul in Manchester, had been arrested at his home residence on Whalley Road, Whalley Range, Manchester. Strongly suspected of being a German spy and a danger to the security of Britain, he was interviewed at length and taken to Dyffryn Aled for internment. Once there, he became the mess secretary for the German prisoners, and a more ebullient man it would surely have been difficult to find!

A less than flattering portrait of Schlagintweit can be found in the book *Set Down in Malice: A Book of Reminiscences*, published in 1919, shortly after the end of the First World War. It was written by Gerald Cumberland, the pseudonym of Charles Frederick Kenyon, a journalist and music critic who lived from 1877 to 1926. When reading this book, despite never having seen a likeness of

Schlagintweit, one cannot help but picture his build and character as being rather like that of Hermann Wilhelm Goering, the German flying ace of the First World War who became the portly, grinning henchman of Hitler. Could any man ever smile with so much inherent malice as Goering? The following extract is taken from pages 159 to 161 of Cumberland's book, and it concerns a time just before the First World War:

My native town is young and strenuous and guileless. Its vanity is the vanity of the clever youngster who loves 'showing off' in his exuberant way. So young and guileless is it, that it is the easiest thing in the world to deceive it. How easy it is to deceive Manchester is illustrated by the case of Captain Schlagintweit, the German Consul for some years in that city.

Schlagintweit was an enormous German whose mission in life was to induce Manchester to believe that Germany was our bosom friend, that Germany's first thought was to help Great Britain, and that the two peoples were so closely akin in their spiritual aims that a quarrel between them, even a temporary misunderstanding, was utterly and forever impossible. As I have said, he was enormous: a great man with a fair round belly: a man who talked and ate a lot, and who, when he talked even with a solitary companion, spoke as though he were addressing a large audience. He 'bounded' beautifully, and with so much aplomb and zest that it seemed right he should bound and do nothing else.

I met him everywhere – in the Press Club, at concerts, at the Schiller Anstalt[1], in restaurants, and nine times out of ten

---

[1] The Schiller-Anstalt was a German club in Manchester for the many German-born or German-connected residents of the city. It was named in honour of the German poet, philosopher, playwright and historian, Frederick Schiller. In this context, 'Anstalt' is the German word for establishment.ain Theodore Schlagintweit

he was in the company of either a journalist, a member of the city council, or a member of parliament. I never knew of any man who worked so hard for his country as he did. He distilled sweet poison into our ears and we believed him every time.

I must confess I felt rather flattered by the way in which he constantly sought my company. I thought for a long time that he loved me for my own sweet sake, and it was not until the, for him, tragic denouement came that I realised it was because I was a journalist, and for that reason alone, he dined and wined me and talked discreetly of Germany's heartache for Great Britain. As I very rarely wrote on international politics, I do not think that his evil counsel had any appreciable effect on my work, but it is impossible to imagine that his overflowing bonhomie, his cleverness, his subtle scheming did not greatly influence the thoughts of Manchester. He was made much of by more than one member of the Manchester Guardian staff.

His daughter came to sing at a concert I organised and it was only after this that he so overwhelmed me with flattery that I looked at him in amazement. I said to myself: 'You are a humbug.' But on looking at him again I said: 'No, you're not a humbug, you're a fool.' A third scrutiny however left me in doubt and I said: 'I'm damned if I know what you are.' Certainly, I never suspected he was first cousin to a Spy, that he was paid handsomely by his Government for his propaganda work in Manchester, and that he secretly despised and hated us.

Shortly after War broke out, many things were discovered about Schlagintweit that had hither-to been unknown, and he was led, handcuffed, to Knutsford Gaol, but not before he had broken through the five-mile radius to which, as a German, he was confined, and not before he had motored through a far-off district where tents of thousands of our soldiers were encamped.

I do not believe London would have been deceived by him, and I am sure Ecclefechan wouldn't, yet Manchester was.

Manchester is young, ingenuous, trusting, guileless.

The bellicose British publication *John Bull* had, by early October 1914, got wind of a scandal brewing in Manchester over the alleged cosy relationship between the now interned Captain Theodore Schlagintweit and certain 'notables' of Manchester society. The *Denbighshire Free Press* published the following on the matter in their Saturday, 17 October 1914 edition:

THE MANCHESTER CONSUL

We had an extract one week from 'John Bull', as to an enquiry held in Manchester as to the close connection between the Chairman of the Watch Committee (a Council committee that oversaw policing and public lighting in their county borough), the Chief Constable and Captain Schlagintweit, the former Manchester Consul, who is now a prisoner at Dyffryn Aled. Councillor Ross Clynes made his statement at Wednesday's Council. The Chairman briefly, but comprehensively denied all the charges made and only three members of the Council voted for Mr Clynes' 'Vote of Censure', with 84 against. The Salford Council we note, have struck the name of the ex-Consul off the vice-presidency in connection with the Technical Institute.

This next account of Captain Theodore Schlagintweit appeared in the Saturday, 6 March 1915 edition of the *Denbighshire Free Press* newspaper, when Schlagintweit was en route back to Germany as part of an exchange deal:

GERMAN CONSUL LEAVES DYFFRYN ALED

Captain Schlagintweit, the ex-German Consul at Manchester, has left the concentration camp at Dyffryn Aled, near Denbigh (where he has been interned six months), presumably for the Fatherland. The Captain who is known as a customer to a number of Denbigh tradesmen, called on some of these on his way from the camp to bid adieu.

At Denbigh Railway Station he was accosted by a young lady who asked him to buy a 'flag', it being the National Flag Day. He politely refused, but relenting, he turned back and deposited a shilling in the girl's collecting box. He has been well treated here and so have his fellow prisoners. If our men in Germany had the same treatment they would be in a different condition to what they are.

Many local enquiries were made, why this man was allowed to leave and the answer was given in the House of Commons on Wednesday evening when Mr Neil Primrose informed Mr Joynson-Hicks that Captain Schlagintweit, the late German Consul in Manchester, had been released after internment for some months. He was one of 12 German Consular officials detained in the United Kingdom whose exchange was recently agreed to for the equivalent number of British officials and other civilians detained in Germany.

The *Liverpool Daily Post* edition of the previous day, Friday, 5 March 1915, had pretty much the same content as the previous article, but had in addition this:

The Captain left without an escort. Before the war the Captain was extremely popular in Manchester, being one of the most genial of men.

The article below appeared the following year in, amongst other Antipodean newspapers, New Zealand's Tuesday, 20 June 1916 edition of the *Poverty Bay Herald*:

SENT HOME TO DRILL HUNS
GERMAN CONSUL WHO MAY HAVE BEEN A SPY

News has reached Manchester through a neutral country that Captain Theodore Schlagintweit, the former German Consul in Manchester, is now actively engaged in drilling Bavarian troops to fight against England.

Captain Schlagintweit was German Consul in Manchester until war broke out. When the first round-up of enemy aliens took place, Captain Schlagintweit was allowed to remain at large, and he had been convicted of a breach of the 'Defence of the Realm Act' by travelling beyond the permitted distance.

He was then sent to the Officers' camp at Dyffryn Aled, in Denbighshire, where he was made mess secretary, and lived in comfort for some months. He was so much at home that he declared that the camp enjoyed 'everything we could desire – except caviar'.

He was released for no known reason in March 1915, and returned to his native land where he was a reserve officer of the Bavarian Rifles.

During his consulship in Manchester, Captain Schlagintweit made friends with all kinds of people who were willing to accept his lavish hospitality. While some of his acquaintances averred that he was a man of the most inoffensive, childlike, and bland type, there were others who regarded him as one of the subtlest of German spies.

It would be interesting to know why he was allowed to go home during the war.

The answer to the question posed at the end of the above is, as a previous newspaper article intimated, that Captain Schlagintweit was exchanged for a British official or officials of equal status. Quite a number of these types of exchanges took place, and while they were generally kept secret by the British authorities, this one got out into the public domain! There were two main reasons for keeping them secret, the first being that the morale of the country would suffer if the public were to learn interned subjects of military or governmental status had been allowed to return to Germany and help in the war effort. The second reason was that the families of many British civilians interned in Germany, and even more so the families of POWs in Germany, would have clamoured for their loved ones to be 'exchanged' also.

A debate in the House of Lords on Thursday, 29 June 1916 concerned un-interned 'enemy aliens'. During it, our old friend Captain Schlagintweit was spoken of as a sort of twentieth-century German Scarlet Pimpernel. Lord St Davids spoke in the debate, and this is an extract from his contribution:

> *Here is a case which was reported in several of the London newspapers the other day. A Captain Theodore Schlagintweit was German Consul in Manchester until the war broke out. When enemy aliens were first rounded up, he was left at large. Eventually he was interned, but he was not interned until he had been convicted of a breach of the 'Defence of the Realm Act' by travelling beyond his permitted distance. He was then sent to a camp in Denbighshire. He was released, for no known reason, in March 1915, and then he returned to Germany. He was a Reserve officer in the Bavarian Rifles, and he is now engaged in drilling Germans to fight this country. That is a pretty strong case.*

Further speculation in the press about Captain Theodore Schlagintweit persisted for well over a year after he had been exchanged. An example of this was a piece in the Saturday, 2 September 1916 edition of the *Denbighshire Free Press*:

A FORMER PRISONER AT DYFFRYN ALED – CONSUL OR SPY?

The Daily Dispatch asks and answers the above questions thus: Was Schlagintweit, the former German Consul in Manchester (who was for some months interned at Dyffryn Aled and then for some reason allowed to depart to Germany), a spy in the employ of the Kaiser's Government?

There is little doubt from the reliable information, which is not advisable to disclose at present, that he was. He is now a Major in the German Army drilling troops. There is a story that he has seen service in France and that the British soldiers captured by Bavarian regiments have been paraded before the ex-Consul.

The plausible Major was one of Germany's greatest and craftiest conspirators, and made full use of his 30 years' residence in Great Britain. For under the guise of the consular office, he was not far removed from being the head – if he was not the actual head – of the spy system out of London.

There is little need to recall his life in Manchester – his lavish expenditure which could not be explained by his modest business standing. Though he was accustomed to talk of his estates in Bavaria, there is no doubt he was subsidised liberally by the German Secret Service. His hospitality therefore was part of the game.

It was also an item of his astute policy to be ever extolling peace relations between England and Germany, and to exalt the Kaiser's peace-loving wishes. And of course, many people

*in Manchester took him at his word. He did his work well
and must indulge in many a grim chuckle to-day as he recalls
his posturing – and his dupes.*

*In Manchester, he quietly surrounded himself with many
former members of the German Army.*

Theodore Schlagintweit, born in Cham Oberpfalz, Bavaria, Germany, on 11 November 1866, was a most interesting and complex character. In 1889, while living in Scotland, he married Glasgow-born Margaret Isabella Reid, and in 1891 they moved to 64 East Clyde Street, Helensburgh, Dumbartonshire. According to the 1901 Census, the Schlagintweit family had moved again, this time to 15 University Gardens Terrace, Hillhead, Glasgow. He would describe himself on paper as simply being a chemical merchant, though in reality he was manager for the Glasgow merchants and chemical brokers, Bryce & Rumpff. The 1911 Census shows that the family had officially come to reside at 94 Market Street in Manchester, with Theodore Schlagintweit now not only a chemical merchant, but also the Imperial German Consul for the city. Their Scottish-born daughter, Therese, birthdate 21 January 1892, aged then nineteen, was a student at the Royal College of Music. Theodore Schlagintweit put a note on his Census form that their private address was 'Wignell', Whalley Road, Whalley Range, Manchester. He was very active in several local groups and societies, and occasionally spoke at the University of Manchester and at the Manchester Geographical Society.

Something intriguing about Theodore Schlagintweit is that on 26 March 1914, he was Initiated into the Cornwall Legh (Masonic) Lodge Number 3382, Sale, Cheshire. He was passed to the Second Degree on 23 April 1914, and Raised to the Sublime Degree of a Master Mason on 28 May

1914. The Cornwall Legh Lodge Number 3382 was founded and consecrated in 1909, and named after the wealthy, landowning Cornwall Legh family of High Legh, near Knutsford, Cheshire. One must question if Theodore Schlagintweit became a member of this Lodge for genuine, altruistic reasons, or merely to further inveigle himself into the British establishment, and those he perceived to be the 'movers and shakers' in the Cheshire and Manchester areas. After all, one of the Cornwall Legh family, Herbert Cornwall Legh, was a founder and leading member of this Lodge, and Schlagintweit only joined Freemasonry in 1914!

The Bavarian WW1 personnel rosters show that Theodore Schlagintweit did indeed re-join the Bavarian Army on his return to Germany, after his time interned at Dyffryn Aled.

Therese Schlagintweit, the Glasgow-born daughter of Theodore Schlagintweit, lived for many years in New Jersey, the United States. She died in 1974, aged eighty-two, in Dallas, Texas.

Chapter Five

Escape from Dyffryn Aled

The first 'successful' escape from Dyffryn Aled by POWs, or at least the first to become public knowledge, took place in the early hours of 5 April 1915. On the evening of 4 April 1915, all prisoners had answered to the roll call, but at 3.00 a.m. the following day, two of them were discovered to be missing. Many local and national newspapers eagerly carried the story in their 6 April 1915 editions and onwards.

The military and civilian authorities had been informed of the escape at once, and using motor cars they scoured the countryside around Dyffryn Aled. The main roads leading from Abergele and Denbigh towards the sea coast and those towards the large industrial towns were watched, and the details and descriptions of the two German officer escapees were widely circulated in the press:

1. Leutnant von Sandersleben, aged about twenty-four, 5 feet 9 inches tall, fresh complexion, brown hair, brown eyes and solidly built, weighing about thirteen to fourteen stones. He was believed to have been wearing at the time of his escape a grey Donegal tweed knickerbocker suit and he was said to be able to speak very little English.

2. Oberleutnant Hans Andler, aged twenty-eight, 5 feet 7 inches tall, of medium build, having dark hair and grey eyes. He was believed to be dressed in a brown suit and was known to be able to speak English fluently. He had only recently been rescued from the North Sea and was said to be an aviator.

The authorities firmly believed that the two men would stay together, as the non-English speaking fugitive would otherwise be easily recaptured. A reward of £10 was offered for information leading to their recapture, a quite tidy sum in those days. Motorists in the area were warned to be wary of any strangers they saw and not to give lifts. The authorities were very confident that the two German officer fugitives would still be near Dyffryn Aled, but wisely extended the search area. Motor garages were warned that the men might try to obtain a vehicle, and all trains were searched as it was believed the men would try to reach one of the cities of England, where German friends could be found to aid them.

Several well-intentioned but totally false sightings of the two men were reported to the authorities. The one most believed to be credible (but in fact incorrect), was a report to the Denbighshire Constabulary of two men answering the descriptions given out. They were seen in a 'worn-out' condition at Ruabon Railway Station at about 5.00 p.m. on 6 April, and had enquired about the next train for London, which they were informed would leave at 5.47 p.m. The pair had boarded and the police believed their destination to be Paddington Station. The train travelled in two sections, and a large force of plain clothes detectives awaited its arrival, but there was no sign to be found of the two fugitives. A thorough search had also been made of both sections of the train at Leamington, also without success.

As days passed, the newspapers began to speculate about the circumstances of the escape, as well as to the suitability of Dyffryn Aled as an internment camp for such resourceful German officer POWs. One such article appeared in *The Times* on Saturday, 10 April 1915, and made mention of 'our friend' Captain Theodore Schlagintweit, the former German Consul in Manchester:

THE ESCAPED OFFICERS
SUGGESTED COMPLICITY OF A FORMER CONSUL
(From our Special Correspondent)
Denbigh, April 9.

The Denbighshire Police are still receiving reports of
mysterious people seen in suspicious circumstances in various
districts within easy reach of Llansannan, but so far as the
fugitive German officers are concerned they are as much in
the dark now as they were on Monday night.

That the escape was carefully planned and was assisted
from outside seems almost beyond question. The fact that
one of the men left money behind him to settle the bill for his
week's laundry seems to leave no doubt that this was not a
sudden decision to make use of an unexpected opportunity.
Locally there is a growing opinion that the escape was
influenced to some extent by Captain Schlagintweit,
formerly German Consul at Manchester, who after a period
of internment at Llansannan was included in a batch of
prisoners returned to Germany about a month ago.
Lieutenant Ambler [sic] is said to be regarded in Germany
as a valuable member of the Flying Corps.

The camp seems to be a comparatively easy one from
which to escape. Until the house itself is reached a visitor is
not challenged and from the road it would be quite possible
to signal to the prisoners in their 'cage' without being seen by
the sentries. Moreover, there are three men in the camp who
have given their parole not to escape and have free access to
the roads and villages in the district.

For all the press speculation and reported sightings of the
two fugitives, von Sandersleben and Andler were actually
recaptured in the village of Talsarnau, near Harlech, then in
the old county of Merionethshire. The sentries who were on

guard duty when the two German officer POWs escaped were put under detention, pending further enquiries.

Despite the two escapees being recaptured, the search for them had not exactly gone smoothly, as this short piece in the *Dundee Courier* of Monday, 12 April 1915 attested:

> *A company of soldiers were engaged on Saturday scouring the mountains near Capel Curig for the two German Officers who escaped from Denbigh, when a heavy mist came on, with the result that the company became scattered, and a number of men lost their way. Some managed to strike a path, which led them to the main road, and others found billets. Most of them have since returned to headquarters at Bangor.*

An account of the recapture of the POWs and the immediate aftermath appeared in the Saturday, 17 April 1915 edition of the *Denbighshire Free Press*:

> *On Sunday afternoon news was conveyed to the Free Press Office of the capture of the escaped German officers from Dyffryn Aled.*
>
> *A telephone message received by Sergeant Evans at the Denbigh Lock-up from Police-constable Davies, of Harlech, stated that it was believed that the two men were then in the cells.*
>
> *Superintendent Woollam, of Denbigh, who has most keenly been following up the clues started at this end of the district, and has had all the men on alert, had gone in a car to Blaenau Festiniog 'on the hunt', and the Sergeant took speedy means of communicating with his Chief, who had also received 'the tip', and had gone on to Harlech, where he arrived soon after the capture by the police there.*
>
> *The two German officers, Lieut. Von Sandersleben (24), and Ober-Lieut. Hans von Andler (28), who escaped from*

the Dyffryn Aled concentration camp, near Denbigh, a week before, had been run to earth at Llanbedr, near Harlech, in Cardigan Bay.

At three o'clock they were seen by the Llanbedr river watcher Mr J. D. Jones coming down the Nantcol Valley. Jones, who was acting under instructions from Police-constable Davies, Harlech, spoke to them, but they made no reply. Jones then sped along a short cut to Llanbedr and telephoned to Police-constable Davies, who had been reconnoitring all morning on his bicycle, and was just starting for Llanbedr. The constable met them on the road, two miles outside Harlech. Dismounting, he charged them with being the escaped prisoners. One of them, who spoke English fairly well, became enraged, and brandishing his fist in the constable's face, threatened to strike him, as he angrily replied that they were Frenchmen on tour. The constable said that story would not wash, and promptly handcuffed both of them, the prisoners making little resistance, for a few yards behind they could see Jones the river watcher, accompanied by the two sons of M. Robert Richards, a Llanbedr magistrate. They afterwards admitted that they were the escaped prisoners.

A few minutes only had elapsed when a trap came along, which the constable commandeered, and having satisfied himself that the prisoners carried no firearms, he took them both to the police station, accompanied by Jones and Messrs Richards. A search was conducted at the police station, and a letter was found on one of them addressed to Hans von Andler, Concentration Camp, Dyffryn Aled, Llansannan.

Mr W. H. Moore, Harlech, a county magistrate, interviewed the prisoners, and in a conversation with him they admitted their identity, and remarked that in a way they were glad that they had been captured. Discussing their experiences, they concluded that, having regard to the rainy, foggy, and misty weather, they had done very well to elude capture for a week. They were confident they could have made good their escape had the weather been better, or had they been in populous centres, instead of such sparsely populated country as North Wales. In making their way towards Arenig they came across Trawsfynydd artillery depot. They made a detour of the depot, and made their way through mountain defiles to the Merioneth coast. They added that they had only set eyes on half-a-dozen people since their escape. They both wore tweed suits and caps. One had puttees. Their boots were much worn, their clothes very wet, and both were badly in need of a shave. They had about £7 in English money, and asked that some of it be used immediately to buy them boots and clothing. They looked healthy and well, but said they felt very tired from sleeping night after night in the wet fields. In their possession, they had a small haversack and a big parcel in a brown box. The latter contained chocolates, biscuits, tobacco, oranges, jams, a fountain pen, and a notebook. On the last page of the notebook was the following memorandum:

'Boat required for secret service, military. Return within two days. Ample reward for secrecy. – Signed, Booth, Captain.'

Inside the notebook there was also a hand drawn map of North and South Wales, with a chart showing apparently the routes and distances to Ireland and Spain. Another map in the notebook showed the coasts of France and England, with a line drawn from the French coast through Harwich and Llansannan on to the Welsh coast at Porthmadog.

Later in the evening the prisoners were conveyed by a motor-car from Harlech, in the charge of Superintendent Woollam and Inspector Owen to Blaenau Festiniog, where they were locked-up in separate cells. They laughed cheerfully when the big crowd outside the police station groaned and were booing at them.

A Daily Mail special correspondent, who had gone by car

on Sunday afternoon from Denbigh to Harlech, had the following story from 'the leader' of the runaways, Lieutenant Hans von Andler:

'We got away at ten o'clock on the Sunday night, an hour after roll-call. I won't tell you how we got away, but I can tell you it was very easy. Our plan was to make our way to the coast and get a train to Cardiff. From there we hoped to get a steamer in the dark, and we thought we might get away to a country like Spain.

'During the whole of Monday, we only saw one man, who looked like a shepherd. We managed to avoid him before he caught sight of us, and went down a mountain track. Most of that day we spent in a thick forest.

'We wanted to get to the coast quickly on the Monday and catch a train to Cardiff. We knew that the people in these parts would not know of our escape until they saw the newspapers on Tuesday, but we could not make our way, although we had a compass and a map. The country was awful; all mountains. The weather, too, was bad and very cold, but we got good shelter against the stone walls. We went on like this for the rest of the week, and we never saw more than four people altogether. We were careful not to call at any place for food. We never went near a house or cottage.

'Yesterday we were near a military camp where some soldiers were practicing firing. We found a shepherd's hut, broke open the door, made a fire, and spent some time there. I boiled some hot water in a can I found and made some chocolate, and we ate some chocolate and cake. We did not stop there on Saturday, but made our way to this place, where we intended to stay the night in a wood, but, as you see, we were caught.'

He said, 'Life was too monotonous, and it was easy to get away. I hope we shan't be taken back there. Our comrades will smile.'

When the prisoners arrived at Festiniog at night they had a very different reception from that at Harlech. The crowd hooted, and then cheered the police, who hurried the Germans into the police station. Andler's first request was for a bath. Andler told me confidently that the Zeppelins had not got seriously to work and that the war would be over by August.

The prisoners on Monday were before Magistrates. They had slept soundly on Sunday night, and after a shave and a change of clothing they looked healthy and cheerful as they stepped into the dock in a crowded court, Sandersleben limping slightly from a sore foot.

Inspector Owen said the prisoners crossed into Merionethshire from Denbighshire at ten o'clock on Saturday morning. The Merionethshire police were on the qui vive and within 30 hours of their arrival in the county they were arrested. Police-constable Nathaniel Davies, Harlech, who effected the arrest, described it as stated above. Witness, who was in plain clothes, charged them with being the escaped prisoners. Andler, the aviator, who speaks English fluently, replied 'No, no, we are touring Frenchmen.'

Loud laughter in the court, in which the prisoners joined. Proceeding, the witness said Andler waved his hands wildly in the witness' face, and was still protesting when he saw several men approaching them. He put down his hands and said, 'Yes, we are the men. We did not care about the prison camp at all, and of course we escaped. We want to be sent to another camp somewhere near the submarine base.' (more laughter).

On searching them he found they had no weapons except two pocket knives, one of which was a big one in a sheath.

On being searched defendants were found with a parcel containing biscuits, chocolates, jams, etc. Also, notebooks and maps. Andler had £4 in English gold and Leben £3.

The Bench, addressing the prisoners, said they would be remanded pending removal to Dyffryn Aled prison camp. The Bench also highly complimented the Merionethshire police on their smartness in arresting the men in a little over twenty-four hours after their crossing the border from Denbighshire (applause). Mr Jones Morris, the magistrates' clerk said, 'They won't come to Merionethshire again in a hurry, seeing our police are so smart.' (laughter, in which the prisoners joined).

Later in the day the prisoners were brought in motor cars supplied by Mr Edwards the Garage, to Denbigh, in the charge of Superintendent Woollam, who was accompanied by Sergeant Evans and one of the Merionethshire officers. The men were handcuffed. On the car containing the prisoners arriving at Love Lane, a big crowd quickly assembled, but the men were hurried into the cells practically before anyone had a glance at them, and there was, therefore, no demonstration. The two Germans, Lieutenant Hans Andler, the aviator and von Sanders Leben are again prisoners of war in the detention camp at Dyffryn Aled, having been brought back from Denbigh by an escort of 35 soldiers. Up to now when any officers have arrived for internment they have been driven in a car or carriage and pair to the camp instead of having to tramp it like our soldiers do. But this time the two runaways had to foot it the whole distance.

By the mid-day train a new guard put in an appearance at Denbigh. They numbered 35, including officers and NCOs, and belonged to the South Lancashire Reserves. They had come for the purpose of relieving or strengthening the guard up to then on duty at Dyffryn Aled. The men were temporarily billeted, and had lunch at the King's Arms, Vale-Street, and the officers at the Bull Hotel; the Commandant of Dyffryn Aled being present at the station to meet them.

*Andler and von Sandersleben being escorted by guards from the Lock-up,
Love Lane, Denbigh*

The Germans were placed in separate cells on their
arrival at Denbigh, and Sergeant Evans kept watch until
they were handed over to the military. The Colonel
commanding the Llansannan camp paid a visit to the cells
and saw the two men, but did not speak to them. Andler was
in the passage at the time, having been allowed to stretch his
legs under the eyes of the officer on guard. When the escort
put in an appearance and the news leaked out that Andler
and Leben were to be marched the distance of nine miles
along the country roads which led to the camp from
Denbigh, there was a large crowd in Love-Lane. When the
handcuffed prisoners made their appearance, there was no
hostile demonstration. Each prisoner was handcuffed to a
Corporal and was fetched out of the cell by four soldiers. The
whole squad of soldiers were ordered to 'fix bayonets' and
with the prisoners and their guards in the outer, marched off
quickly down Love-Lane and down Swine Market to Lenten
Pool, and up Henllan Street. Immediately the town was left
behind [and] the crowd were turned back by the police. The

march up the hills was continued at a good pace, but Andler and Leben kept well in step, and held on well for the whole of the distance. Andler looked thoroughly dejected on arrival. Only a few school children were in the vicinity of the camp. The recaptured men were taken to a different portion of the building from that they occupied before, and they will probably be kept apart from their fellow-countrymen.

Nothing has transpired as to whether they will be transferred to another place of internment.

Small guards of soldiers have within the last nine days been placed at Henllan, Trefnant and Tremeirchion; but it is not known whether this is the result of the recent escape from Dyffryn Aled or not.

An account of the court-martial proceedings appeared in the Friday, 30 April 1915 edition of *The Cambrian News and Merionethshire Standard*, an extract from which is printed below:

'I wish to know', said Andler, whose case was tried first, 'If I can appeal from this court to a higher court?'

The President replied, 'No.'

Producing voluminous notes in which were scribbled extracts from The Hague Convention, Andler made a protest against the jurisdiction of the court. His objection was that not having given his parole, he was only subject to disciplinary punishment by the Commandant at the camp, or by his immediate superior. 'I wish to bring the following to the notice of the court', he said, 'that in the annexe of The Hague Convention, Article 8, Chap.2, it states that escaped prisoners of war who are retaken are liable to disciplinary punishment, but that Article 12, chap.2. states that prisoners of war liberated on parole and recaptured bearing arms against the Government to which they have pledged their honour, forfeit their right to be treated as prisoners of war and may be put on trial before the courts.' He held that punishment of an officer who did not break his parole was not so severe as that of an officer who did.

The President pointed out that whatever punishment was inflicted on him would be confirmed by General Mackinnon, Commanding the Division and his statement would be considered by that officer. The decision of the court was not final. It was liable to be wiped out altogether or modified. There was no appeal after that. The court overruled the plea of the prisoner.

Captain E. Robinson, 5th Battalion, South Lancashire Regiment, who prosecuted said that Andler's conduct at the camp was described by the Commandant as good...

Leben the second prisoner, proved more obstinate than Andler, refusing to plead and also protested against the constitution of the court.

He was stated to be a Lieutenant in the 242nd Reserve Infantry Battalion of the German Army. Twenty-four years of age and his conduct since his internment was described as good. He appealed, referring to The Hague Convention, declaring that he could only receive disciplinary punishment and that such punishment could only be inflicted by one individual and not by a court. If the word disciplinary was unimportant it would not have been embodied in the Convention. Disciplinary might include any form of punishment up to sentence of death. The President overruled this plea, as in the former case and several witnesses were heard to support the charge.

Captain A. Gain, Adjutant at the camp, said that on April 5th he was informed by the Commandant that two prisoners of war, of whom the accused was one, had escaped. He searched for them all over the camp – in the house and basement. The window bars in the house were examined, search parties sent out into the woods and surrounding country, but without result.

> *Colonel Cattell, the Commandant, said that when the accused did not answer his name, he ordered the roll to be called a second time, but accused was still absent. He ordered a thorough search of the house and precincts, but without result, and he next saw the accused at Denbigh Police Court about 9.30 a.m. on April 13th.*

Sub-Lieutenant (in German: *Oberleutnant*) Hans Andler was subsequently sentenced to twenty-eight days imprisonment without hard labour, to be served in the Chelmsford Detention Barracks, after which he would be sent to the internment camp at Donington Hall[2], Castle Donington, Leicestershire.

To give his full name, Lieutenant (in German: *Leutnant*) Hans Friedrich Rudolf von Sandersleben, for having escaped, was also sentenced to twenty-eight-days imprisonment, again without hard labour, also to be served in the Chelmsford Detention Barracks, following which he was removed to Philberds House[3], Holyport, near

---

[2]   In the Summer of 1915, whilst Hans Andler was interned at Donington Hall, the naval pilot Gunther Pluschow escaped from there and managed to leave British shores. He was the only German POW to achieve this during either of the world wars.

[3]   Philberds House, an internment camp for German POWs, was far more rugged than Dyffryn Aled. It consisted of a large old country mansion with extensive gardens surrounded by a large wall. The German POWs lived in corrugated huts that had been erected in the Old Gardens. I have found that many German POW escapees from around Britain, when recaptured, were sent to Philberds House as a form of punishment. The local pub at Holyport was named 'The Eagle', and was situated on Holyport Street. German officer POWs, when marching past while out on various work parties, were said to have regularly and mischievously saluted the eagle emblem on the pub's sign. As a direct result of this, in 1916 or 1917, the name of the pub was changed to 'The Belgian Arms', to remind German prisoners of the atrocities they had committed in neutral Belgium. Today, the pub is still named 'The Belgian Arms' and is a thriving historic village pub, now over two hundred years old.

Maidenhead, Berkshire. He was not a happy man to say the least, and subsequently made an official protest to the British military authorities about his treatment following his recapture, and concerning the procedure and sentence of the court-martial upon him.

The *Denbighshire Free Press* newspaper Saturday, 8 May 1915 edition had the following observation to make on the press coverage of the two escapees' court-martials:

> *A correspondent in the newspaper world says: 'Frequently journalists experience difficulty in getting admission to courts-martial, but there was a welcome exception in the case of the trial of the two German officers who escaped from Dyffryn Aled Concentration Camp. It was specifically announced that the press would be admitted to the courts-martial. About a dozen journalists were present and reasonable accommodation was provided.'*

It was a sort of 'show trial' before the world, but more especially for the consumption of the British public and the German authorities.

Chapter Six

The Submarine Escape Plan

The second 'successful' escape from Dyffryn Aled took place some four months after the first, and I proffer it was the most audacious of any that took place during the First World War. The Saturday, 21 August 1915 edition of the *Abergele and Pensarn Visitor* had this to say:

> *Shortly before noon on Tuesday, an ambulance belonging to one of the regiments billeted at Llandudno passed through Abergele bearing an interesting load. In the far end of the vehicle was seated Leutnant Hans Werner von Helldorff, Captain Heinrich Julius von Henning [sic], and Captain Hermann Tholens, the three German officers who had escaped from the internment camp at Llansannan on Saturday morning. They were being conveyed back to Dyffryn Aled in the charge of a commissioned officer, a sergeant and three privates of the London Welsh Battalion, all of whom were armed with rifles with fixed bayonets. The trio were handcuffed. Following their escape, the fugitives, according to a statement they made to military officers at Llandudno, wandered about in the uplands, hiding by day and endeavouring to reach the coast by night. Eventually they did at about 8.00 p.m. on Monday, when they reached Llandudno. Tholens, a fluent English speaker, took the lead. Helldorff, who has an imperfect knowledge of English, and Henning [sic], who cannot speak a word of it, followed on behind.*
>
> *Tholens was 'found out' at a tobacconist shop in Mostyn Street by the way he uttered his vowels. Meanwhile, the*

fugitive leader had been shadowed by a police constable, who later approached him with the challenge, 'What nationality are you?' Tholens replied, 'I want to be arrested. I am a Lieutenant in the German Navy and was in command of a submarine.' The Constable remarked that he was the fellow he was looking for and at that the Teuton laughed and was taken into custody. The sum of £28 8s 3d in English money was found upon him. The other fugitives were observed by a cabman who drove up and asked if they wanted a cab. They replied that they did and stepped into the cab. The quick-witted cabman drove them to the H.Q. of the London Welsh Battalion. They were arrested about 45 minutes after Tholens. At Abergele, Colwyn Bay, Rhyl, Denbigh and other centres the Military Authorities were out looking for them. Soldiers with rifles and bayonets searched, and it was believed the three fugitives intended to book a train to London where they would hide out until getting passage out of the country.

The *Denbighshire Free Press* of Saturday, 21 August 1915 carried a similar account of their escape and subsequent recapture at Llandudno, but also included quite detailed descriptions of the three:

Lieutenant Hans Werner von Helldorff, age 29, height 6 feet one and a half inches, small moustache, fair hair, light complexion, medium build, scar on left cheek. Dress believed to be a dark grey uniform. He speaks a little English.

Captain Heinrich Julius von Hennig, age 31, height 5 ft. 10 in., clean shaven, dark hair, brown hair, slight build, believed to be dressed in white naval uniform with plain buttons. He speaks no English.

Captain Hermann Tholens, age 32, height 5 ft. 11 in., light hair, prominent blue-grey eyes, dress believed to be blue naval uniform with plain buttons, clean shaven and with very bald head. He speaks English fluently, but with a German accent.

The military authorities had believed the three German officer fugitives would make for London by train and hide out until they could secure passage out of the country. Well, how very wrong they were. It turned out the three had hatched a far more grandiose and organised plan of escape back to Germany, one which would involve passage by U-Boat, and their plan so very nearly succeeded!

The same Saturday, 21 August 1915 edition of the *Denbighshire Free Press* published the following on the matter, under their St Asaph news section:

AN INTERESTING SIGHT

A covered motor ambulance, said to contain the three officers who escaped from Dyffryn Aled last week, passed through the City [St Asaph] on Tuesday and was the cause of considerable speculation amongst its citizens. The spectacle of several soldiers with fixed bayonets on the ambulance was probably the foundation of the belief. Great disappointment is expressed that no one actually saw the prisoners.

The *Manchester Evening News* edition of Friday, 27 August 1915 carried this detailed account of the court-martials of Tholens, von Hennig and von Helldorff:

GERMAN OFFICERS' ESCAPE WELSH CAMP INCIDENT
MILITARY ENQUIRY AT CHESTER

To-day a Military Court was held at Chester Castle to hear evidence regarding the escape of three German officers from the Dyffryn Aled Prisoners of War Camp, near Denbigh. It will be recalled that the enemy officers disappeared from the internment camp on a Saturday and were recaptured at Llandudno. The officers were:

Lieutenant Hans Werner von Helldors [sic], 29, who was in a smartly cut grey uniform of the German Army. He stands 6 ft. high and had fair hair and is of light complexion and wore a monocle.

Captain N. Hendrick [sic] Julius von Henning [sic], 31, a naval man, wearing a captain's uniform with gold facings. Captain Hermann Tholens, 43, also a naval captain, wearing the uniform of a captain. He stands 5 ft. 11 in.

All the prisoners were well groomed and faultlessly dressed. The court was composed of several officers, Brigadier-General R. Style, of the 119th Infantry Brigade, being president.

The first case heard was that of Captain Tholens, who said his friends and himself had no one to defend them. He was charged that he, being a prisoner of war, committed an offence at Dyffryn Aled Camp on August 13th, by escaping from a place of internment. Asked if he was guilty or not guilty, he replied, 'I am guilty.'

The President: 'You understand that when you plead guilty the court finds you guilty without hearing any evidence?'

Captain Tholens: 'I understand that.'

The President then read over the evidence.

Captain A. Gain, adjutant and quartermaster of the camp, deposed to taking a roll call on August 13 at 7 p.m., when all were present, and Captain Tholens answered his name. Shortly after nine o'clock the following morning, the commandant informed him that three of the German officers were absent. Witness proceeded to the house and was unable to find any of them.

Lieutenant-Colonel Cattell, commandant of the camp, said [that] at 9 a.m. on August 14, he was present at the roll call. Captain Tholens was absent. Witness gave orders for the house and precincts to be searched, and Captain Tholens was not found. Subsequently, the accused was brought back from Llandudno.

Acting Quartermaster-Sergeant Baird deposed to inspecting on August 12th the bars and all means of exit from the house. All were correct, but on the 14th it was found that a bar had been tampered with in No. 2 ward of the West Wing. Lieutenant W. P. Ward deposed to discovering that one of the upright bars in that part of the house had been sawn through in such a way that it was impossible to detect it unless the bar was lifted. All except one-eighth of an inch had been previously sawn through, and it was quite rusty.

The accused was found guilty of the offence.

Asked if he wished to make any statement, the prisoner, speaking in excellent English, said:

'At Llandudno on August 17th, the day after I was captured, we got orders to be sent back to Dyffryn Aled, and the officer of the escort – I do not know his name, came up to me and told me that he was to handcuff us. He said he regretted it very much, as he did not think it was the habit to handcuff officers, but he was bound to do it, as his orders had been very exact and strict. I asked if it could not have been a misunderstanding, but he said "No." Then I offered to give my parole not to escape on the way to Dyffryn Aled. The officer said it was quite impossible for him to take it according to his orders. Thus, we were handcuffed. When we came back to Dyffryn Aled we were kept waiting before the chief entrance – not the entrance we went through before – so that we could be seen not only by all our own officers, but by the soldiers of the guard. We were kept waiting about 15 minutes. Then the colonel, the commanding officer, came up and the only question he asked as he saw us standing guarded in the midst of several armed soldiers was – "Are these officers handcuffed?" I regard this as a degrading indignity against an officer who has been made prisoner fighting in the war.'

When the statement was read over to the accused, he added, regarding the waiting outside the house: 'We could not have been seen if we had gone through the ordinary entrance, which we entered when we first arrived.'

Afterwards the court heard the case against Captain von Henning [sic], for whose case a civilian interpreter was called to translate the evidence.

The Captain explained that he understood English much better than he spoke it. He pleaded guilty, and had nothing to say in answer to the charge.

He was found guilty.

Asked if he wished to make any statement, the accused also complained about being handcuffed, which he regarded as superfluous as they were guarded by one commissioned officer and three men with bayonets, which he thought would have been precaution enough.

The accused added: 'This touched my sentiment of honour, the more so as in Germany only the lowest criminals would be transported like this, and not an officer of the army and navy.'

Accused also stated that he was told it was not according to the rules of the English Army to handcuff officers.

The court afterwards heard the evidence against the third officer and the sentences will be promulgated in due course.

Further to the above account, after lunch, the third accused German officer, Lieutenant Hans Werner von Helldorff, with the assistance of a translator, also pleaded guilty. He said in translation that he was an officer in the German Army and that it was his duty to escape and return home. He too complained that on their return to Dyffryn Aled after recapture, the commanding officer Colonel Cattell had insisted that all three German officers remained handcuffed in front of British soldiers and workmen at the camp. He made a formal complaint as to their treatment, also stating that in Germany only the lowest criminals are handcuffed.

The sentences upon the three were then considered at length by the military court. When their verdicts were promulgated, it was eighty-four days imprisonment without hard labour for each of them, to be served in Chelmsford Detention Barracks, where they were immediately taken from Chester Castle.

From their cells in Chelmsford Detention Barracks, all three wrote official letters of complaint to the British authorities. These regarded their treatment on recapture, and to the procedures of the military court, as well as to the sentences handed down to them.

It was eighteen years later, during the interbellum period, that the *Evening Telegraph* newspaper of Friday, 19 May 1933 prominently featured the below article as part of its 'Adventure of Escape' series. The article is Hermann Tholens' account of how he became a POW and his escape from Dyffryn Aled:

> *I was taken prisoner in the first days of the war, when the German cruisers, Coln, Mainz and Ariadne were sunk during a raid of the English fleet into the Bight of Heligoland on August 28th, 1914.*
>
> *I was second in command of the Mainz, and I was in the water about an hour after she was sunk. I was then picked up by an English destroyer and taken on board. The first ten days of my captivity I passed in the naval hospital at*

Chatham, and from there I was taken to Dyffryn Aled Camp, near Denbigh, right in the north of Wales.

This camp was, I think, one of the best guarded of all the prisoner-of-war camps in the whole of Britain – probably because most of its inmates were Submarine Officers.

My thoughts turned to escape at once, but I am six feet, two inches in height, and this, I believed, would make it difficult for me to move about English ports and dockyards undetected.

So, I decided to try to arrange to leave in much the same way that I had come – that is to say, by means of one of our own ships of war.

The coast of Wales was only a few miles north, and it seemed to me that if only I could break camp and get there, I might arrange for a German Submarine to meet me there and take me off.

This plan for a rendezvous needed, of course, to be very careful and accurate; but I talked it over with a fellow prisoner, my friend Lieutenant-Commander von Hennig, who had been the Captain of our Submarine 18. We made a careful investigation of the camp's defences, and decided that if we could get our Admiralty to send a Submarine to a certain part of the coast at a certain time, we could keep our side of the bargain and be there to meet it.

At Christmas, 1914, some of the prisoners of our camp who had lived in England before the war were exchanged by special arrangement against a like number of English prisoners from Germany.

By one of these I sent a secret proposal to the Commander-in-Chief of the German flotillas.

My proposal was this. My friend von Hennig and I undertook to get out of our camp and reach an agreed point on the Welsh Coast at an agreed time. Would it be possible for one of the Submarines operating in the Irish Sea to be detailed and sent to meet us there?

We proposed the most westerly point of the Great Orme's Head as a rendezvous, and a Saturday and Sunday during a new moon as a time of meeting. Our signal would be an electric pocket lamp waved in a circle. The answer to this proposal was given in several letters, in what I can only call was 'disguised language'. It was really very easy.

The three escapers attempting to signal the U-38, at Great Orme's Head

Our friends thanked us for our letters, and said that the wedding of Mrs So-and-So would take place on August 14th.

We quite understood what was meant, and after a further exchange of letters we knew that a Submarine was to await us at the proposed point during the nights of 14th and 15th of August 1915.

Now for our part of the job – reaching the rendezvous. We must reach it – for a second chance was not to be expected.

And unfortunately, while our negotiations were being made with Germany, the chances to get out of our camp had diminished considerably. In March, two of our fellow prisoners had made a vain escape, with the result that our camp was now guarded during the night by six sentries instead of by two. The equipment of the camp had also been augmented by four searchlights, which were posted at the four corners, and made the nights all round it as light as the days. At the same time, the number of roll-calls had been doubled and extra rolls had been introduced. But where there's a will there's a way. These new orders dated from the middle of June, and according to them the searchlights had to be lighted at 9.00 p.m., which was also the time for the six night guards to take up their stations. Two of them were stationed in front of the house, one at each side, and two again in the back. By the middle of August, the time of our rendezvous, the days of course would have become shorter than they were in June, when the above order had been issued.

So, we agreed that the best time for our breaking away from camp would be a little before the searchlights were lighted, and the night guards took up their stations, as it would be already pretty dark then.

Our plan was this. We intended to get through the iron-barred windows of the room which was inhabited by my two fellow-escapers, for we had added by now a third to our number.

Our next obstacle was the first of the two entrance gates, which led through the barbed wire fence which surrounded our prison. If the gate could not be opened, we should have to cut the barbed wire fence next to the room from which we started, and endeavour to crawl through it.

Thus, our preparations had to consist of cutting one of the iron window bars and in removing the hanging lock from the aforesaid entrance gate as soon as possible before the time for our escape.

On the date of our escape everything was in order, and nobody except us had the least idea about our intentions.

At 7 o'clock in the evening we were in possession of the hanging lock of the entrance gate, and by 8.30 it had not yet been replaced by a new one. Sharply at 8.41 we stole through our window, crawled very, very slowly to our gate, only twenty yards from the nearest sentry, and one or two minutes later we were outside the camp.

Half an hour before we left, we had informed our trusted friends of our intention, and they promised to help us. One of them was to replace the cut iron bar and the other distracted the attention of the sentry who was stationed in front of the house by troubling him with some very important questions. We had to cover about twenty miles to reach our meeting place. And this had to be done within the next twelve hours, as we should certainly be missed at the daily roll-call, which took place at 9 o'clock in the morning, and then, of course, the telephones would work and soon all authorities in the neighbourhood would know that three prisoners of war of Dyffryn Aled were at large.

At 6.30 we reached the seaboard. A very supreme moment! A little later we entered the town of Llandudno. We strolled along the streets, crossed a large training field in the middle of the town and admired at our leisure the exercises and drilling of a whole army of soldiers.

Before leaving the town, we resolved to have a last good English breakfast. We took this in a nice little restaurant near the sea. Then we set off again, and soon made our way to the lighthouse on Great Orme's Head. When we reached this, we looked for a nice spot where we could shelter all the day and perhaps the following day too. For we had arranged, you remember, that the Submarine should wait for us on two consecutive nights.

On August 4th, Submarine 38 left Wilhelmshaven to meet us, and took her course through the North Sea to the Shetlands, where she arrived two days later. From there she sailed through the Atlantic, along the West Coast of Scotland and Ireland, into the Channel, and then into the Irish Sea.

Great Orme's Head and lighthouse, Llandudno

South of Ireland she sank some hostile ships with contraband. But in the Irish Sea she made no further attacks in order not to arouse unnecessary suspicion. At midnight on August 13th she had reached a point fifty miles North West of Great Orme's Head, where she had to await Submarine 27, which had been sent for the same purpose and to make it as sure as possible that one boat would be ready for us at the fixed time.

Here, the Captain of Submarine 38, who was a special friend of ours, proposed that the other boat should return to her business in the mouth of the Channel, as from now on one boat would be sufficient.

Submarine 27, therefore, went off to the South, while next evening, August 14th, Submarine 38 slowly approached the Hook of Great Orme's Head; when she sounded about thirty yards, she put off her diesel motors and put on the electric engines. At the same time, the boat was flooded – that is to say, some of her tanks were filled with water, so that if she grounded, she could get up again by blowing out the water.

The weather and the sea were quiet. There was no traffic and no patrol boat. At one o'clock in the morning she sounded ten yards and stopped her engines. The lamp on the lighthouse on Great Orme's Head showed very high up. The distance from shore could not be more than a hundred yards. But the rocks of the coast could not be made out as it was absolutely dark. All the crew was intently on the look-out, but no sign of life could be perceived. The small collapsible boat of the submarine was all the while kept ready to row ashore. Hour by hour passed, but nothing happened.

Now to return to us. At 10 o'clock on the night of the 14th, when it was absolutely dark, we left our shelter beneath a couple of brambles, and carefully made our way to a point which we had marked in the morning, where it would be possible to climb down the high rocky cliffs of the Coast.

But in the dark we missed the place and could not find our way down. If any of you know the Great Orme's Head, you will remember that it is a very difficult place to climb down on a dark night.

So, we resolved to give our signal from above this night, rather than to risk some broken arms or legs and so perhaps spoil our chances of being taken on board by our friends on the following night.

It must be understood that as well as the difficulties and dangers of the rocks, we were also in great danger of being detected by the coastguards, who were constantly patrolling the road which led along the cliff and round the lighthouse. At daybreak on the Sunday we carefully revised our position and especially the possibilities to climb down to the shore.

We found that our position was right. We were on the most westerly point of Great Orme's Head, just halfway between the last houses which bordered the coast, and the lighthouse.

Our distance from the lighthouse which was in the most

northerly point of the coast, was no more than a thousand yards. But the part of the coast between us and the lighthouse was extremely rocky. So, we again carefully marked the spot, from which we would be able to clamber down to the shore. This was our last chance; we were not going to miss it, a second time.

Then we took up our quarters again in our small nest beneath the brambles and tried to sleep a little. But our excitement was too great, and sleep was impossible. We left our shelter before it was dark and got safely down to the coast. At 10 o'clock we began to give our signals – a circle with our electric lamp.

It was a wonderful night, I remember – absolutely dark, with no moon. The sea was quiet, and only a slight breeze was blowing. If the submarine was there – surely she was there – she would certainly make out our signals at a distance of at least two miles. But we got no answer.

We began to think that she must have had some mishap and had not been able to reach the rendezvous on time. If need be, we would wait for her a third night in our hunger and thirst – but meanwhile we flashed and flashed our light. There was no reply.

In desperation, we then risked making a large fire from bits of drift wood from the shore, and every ten minutes during the last hour of darkness we waved a large log of flaming wood in a circle. We made our signals as far north as the rocky coast allowed, but no answer came.

How disappointed we were! I can't put that into words at all. We hid again when day broke, intending rather hopefully to try again the next night. But we had to give up the plan, for a strong gale from the north sprang up in the afternoon, and soon the sea was too rough to make any such embarkation possible.

What had happened?

During the day, the submarine had lain grounded some miles away. On that Sunday, she had come to the surface again and approached the coast. The Captain, our friend Valentiner, knew from the previous night that there was no danger from patrol boats, so he approached the shore this time early enough to get as close to it as possible.

That was our bad luck. For they had been waiting for us, but closer in than we'd expected and just hidden from us by a projecting ledge of rock. It had been waiting for us there, not more than 100 yards away, but had not been able to see our signals.

In the evening, after the gale had made it useless to wait for the submarine a third night, I left my friends who couldn't speak English. My intentions were to reach London and smuggle on board some Dutch or Scandinavian vessel.

But at the station of Llandudno, a Policeman stopped me. He said I looked very like a certain Lieutenant-Commander Tholens who had escaped from Dyffryn Aled three days before.

I could only answer, 'Right you are.'

'Our friend Valentiner', as he is named in the above account, was the U-Boat commander of the *U-38*. His full name was Christian August Max Ahlmann Valentiner, better known as Max Valentiner. He was born on 15 December 1883 at Tondern, Schleswig-Holstein. In April 1902, he joined the Imperial German Navy as a sea cadet (in German: *seekadett*), being promoted to acting sub-lieutenant (in German: *leutnant zur see*) in 1905, then to sub-lieutenant in 1908, captain-lieutenant on 22 March 1914, and to corvette captain in 1918.

During the First World War, Max Valentiner held two separate U-Boat commands: *U-38* from 5 December 1914 to 15 September 1917, and then the new *U-157* from 22

Max Valentiner, U-Boat Commander

September 1917 to 20 July 1918. For his distinguished naval service and leadership, he was awarded a number of medals, including the Iron Cross 2nd Class, the Iron Cross 1st Class, and the *Pour Le Merite* (in English: For Merit), better known as 'The Blue Max'. As a U-Boat commander in the First World War, he had a very high 'success record':

Ships sunk:	143
Warships sunk:	1
Ships damaged:	5
Warships damaged:	1
Ships taken as prizes:	3

Though Max Valentiner was a great hero of Germany, he was to Britain and its Allies nothing more than a despised 'pirate and war criminal', not only because of his successful naval record, but due to his torpedoing, without warning, of the SS Persia, a P. & O. passenger liner, on 30 December 1915. This civilian ship sank very quickly, with the loss of 343 out of 519 souls on-board.

Max Valentiner died in hospital at Sonderborg, Denmark, on 19 July 1949. The cause of his death was lung disease, said to have been the direct result of inhaling toxic vapours from the engines of the earlier U-Boat models on which he had served.

One thing which Hermann Tholens had not shared while writing of his escape attempt was the fate of the other U-Boat involved. The *U-27* had been commissioned on 8 May 1914, and its commander was Captain (in German: *Kapitan*) Bernard Wegener. Over the course of a mere three patrols, it had been responsible for the sinking of ten merchant ships and two warships. After its rendezvous with the *U-38* on 13 August 1915, the *U-27* went back on the hunt, but only six days later, on 19 August 1915, it was itself the target of gunfire from the British 'Q Ship', *Baralong*, in the Western Approaches. All thirty-seven of the *U-27*'s crew, including Captain Wegener, were killed.

Allegedly, Lieutenant-Commander Godfrey Herbert on the *Baralong* had ordered that instead of rescuing the ten to twelve (the figure varies by accounts) survivors of the *U-27* and taking them as POWs, they should be killed as they struggled in the water, in essence executing them on the spot! The British Admiralty went to great lengths to suppress this dark tale, but it spread to Germany, where it was (and still is) referred to as 'the infamous *Baralong* Incident'.

If the allegations regarding the actions of the commander and crew of the *Baralong* are true, one should be mindful that this 'incident' took place only three months after the infamous and merciless sinking of the *RMS Lusitania* by the German U-Boat, the *U-20*, resulting in the loss of a staggering 1,198 passengers – many of them women and children.

Barely six years after the publication in Britain of Hermann Tholens' account of escape and recapture, Britain and Germany were at war again, this time on an even more global scale, and with far higher military and civilian casualties than occurred in 'the war to end all wars'. Hermann Tholens and other former 'inmates' of Dyffryn Aled from the First World War, now in their forties and fifties, were once again called upon to fight for their Fatherland, but instead of fighting for Emperor Wilhelm II and Imperial Germany, they now fought, many in senior positions, for the nefarious Hitler. These former 'Dyffryn Aled' men very much became part of the 'Nazi war machine'.

Chapter Seven

Other Escape Attempts

Escape by tunnel

On 10 May 1916, news reached nearby Denbigh that a bold escape attempt had been made by some German officer POWs at Dyffryn Aled. The method used by these men had been tunnel, which was ingenious given that it would be twenty-seven years before the vaunted 'Great Escape' by British and Allied POWs at Stalag Luft III.

The facts were that several German officer POWs had dug an eight-foot-deep shaft under the storeroom in the north-west wing. At the bottom of it, they had created a tunnel fifteen yards in length, bringing their excavations to within a few feet of the laurel plantation outside of the compound. The discovery of the tunnel by those in charge of Dyffryn Aled was rather timely, as it had been close to completion.

A great deal of excavation work went into the building of the escape tunnel, and it must have taken the POWs some months to reach the stage they had, as the tunnel was rather narrow and only allowed one at a time to carry out excavation. The discovery of the tunnel was widely talked about in the district and became something of a sensation. Much satisfaction was expressed in the local press that the attempt of the 'Huns' to escape had been frustrated.

William Le Queux

The Sunday Post of Sunday, 30 September 1917 featured a long, bitterly worded article by William Le Queux, the writer and lecturer who had foretold of a coming war with Germany long before 1914, a stance which was often derided in the pre-First World War days. The article bore the headline 'SCANDAL OF ESCAPING GERMAN PRISONERS' and the sub-heading of 'SEQUEL TO PETTING PIRATES – DEMAND FOR DRASTIC MEASURES'. Le Queux regularly wrote of the 'hidden hand' of German influence still in Britain, particularly London. He also deplored the frequency with which German POWs were escaping from internment camps in Britain. Le Queux alluded to the fact that a number of these escapees could live and go about openly for days and weeks in cities because they were aided by fellow Germans still at large. Le Queux's words were robust, but basically it was the truth that he was telling.

Six more escape from Dyffryn Aled

In the late evening of 10 April 1918, or in the early hours of 11 April 1918, five German officers and one of their servants escaped from Dyffryn Aled. The press dubbed it generally as 'Hun's Bid for Escape'. Four of the escaping German officers travelled together inland, one 'lone wolf' officer made for the west coast of Wales, and the servant headed for the town of Rhyl.

The *Denbighshire Free Press* newspaper of Saturday, 13 April 1918, reported the following upon the capture of the four German officers who had travelled together:

CAPTURE OF ESCAPED GERMAN PRISONERS

Considerable excitement was caused in Ruthin on Thursday morning when it became known that four German prisoners of war, who had escaped from Dyffryn Aled Internment Camp the previous day, had been captured and brought to the town. Notice of the escape had been received by Inspector Harvey and he was abroad at an early hour on the lookout for the fugitives. Not long afterwards the Inspector came across the four, took charge of the prisoners and conveyed them to the lock-up at Ruthin. Two of their companions who escaped with them, are still at large. Information regarding their capture was given to the military authorities and an escort arrived later in the day and removed them.

The 'lone wolf' German escaper did considerably better than the other five. The following is an account of his recapture which appeared in the *North Wales Chronicle* of Friday, 19 April 1918:

GERMAN OFFICER'S ESCAPE FROM DYFFRYN ALED CAMP

Late on Tuesday night a German officer prisoner of war from Dyffryn Aled Camp, Denbighshire, who escaped early on Thursday morning was caught near the famous Cwmbychan Lake, a few miles from Barmouth. He had been out on the Welsh mountains for five nights and suffered greatly from exposure and was very hungry. He called at a farmhouse and asked for a night's lodgings, stating he had lost his way in the mountains. His wife, he said, was staying on holiday at Barmouth and he was an American citizen. The farmer gave information to Police Constable Nathaniel Davies, of Harlech, and the German was taken into custody.

The *Hull Daily Mail* of Wednesday, 17 April 1918 had this version of events regarding the 'lone wolf' German officer escaper:

ESCAPED GERMANS CAPTURED

The German Officer, Karl Wilhelm Heinrich Hoch, 36, who

escaped from Dyffryn Aled last Friday, was captured by John Lloyd of Harlech, a discharged soldier and manganese worker, on the mountains above Cwmbychan Lake and the famous Roman Steps. The other German officers who were with him when he escaped were recaptured in Ruthin, and one near Rhyl.

The following is from the Friday, 3 May 1918 edition of *The Cambrian News* and *Merionethshire Standard*:

POLICE CONSTABLE COMPLIMENTED

The Chairman on behalf of the Justices complimented P.C. Nathaniel Davies, Harlech, on the way he arrested the escaped German officer this month [April]. This is the third time that P.C. Davies has captured German prisoners. He also wished to thank the civilians who gave valuable assistance to the constable. P.C. Davies then thanked the Justices.

The due diligence of Police Constable Nathaniel Davies of Harlech, known as 'Nath', was duly rewarded when, in the *North Wales Chronicle* of Friday, 11 April 1919, the Chief Constable of Merionethshire, Mr Richard Jones, announced promotions and transfers within his force. They included P.C. Nathaniel Davies, who was promoted to Sergeant at Blaenau Ffestiniog.

A meal on the lawn!
This account of the recapture of two German officer POWs, who had made their escape from Dyffryn Aled on 2 June 1918, appeared in the Saturday, 8 June 1918 edition of the *Denbighshire Free Press*:

HOW TWO GERMAN PRISONERS WERE RECAPTURED

Two German prisoners of war escaped on Sunday from the Internment Camp at Dyffryn Aled. At mid-day on Tuesday, two strangers went into the grocery stores and post office at Llanfynydd, near Hope, Flintshire, occupied by Mr Jonathan Hurst. There chanced to be in the shop at the same time a commercial traveller, who addressing the strangers in German said, 'You are German prisoners.' One of the men in reply said, 'You need not be afraid. We are done-up and want something to eat.' Mr Hurst communicated with the police and Superintendent Connah arrived in a motor car to find the two Germans sitting at a table on the lawn at the rear of the premises enjoying a substantial meal. They admitted they were the wanted fugitives and were taken back in the Superintendent's car to Mold. They stated that since their escape they had walked chiefly along the main roads and that they passed through the town of Mold at midnight on Monday. One of them vouchsafed the information that he had been a prisoner of war for exactly twelve months. The camp authorities were apprised of their recapture.

The final escape from Dyffryn Aled

Escapes and escape attempts by German officers from Dyffryn Aled continued right up to the Armistice on Monday, 11 November 1918. The following account appeared in the *Liverpool Daily Post* on Thursday, 24 October 1918:

ESCAPE FROM WELSH CAMP

Lieutenant Franz Lane, a German officer, aged 21, escaped on Tuesday from the camp at Bynwryn [sic], near Abergele. The officer, who speaks a little English, is described as of sallow complexion, brown hair, blue-grey eyes, and slim build. He is 5 ft. 10 in. in height, and was dressed in field-grey uniform.

The *Denbighshire Free Press* of Saturday, 2 November 1918 had this on Franz Lane's recapture:

ESCAPED GERMAN OFFICER RE-TAKEN

A German officer named Franz Lane, who had been missing from Dyffryn Aled Camp nearly a week, was quietly arrested in the streets of Carnarvon. Despite the darkness, Sergeant Jones made up his mind that a tall young man who had passed him in the street answered the description given of the fugitive and upon going to him, the latter quietly turned around and said, 'It is alright, Sergeant.' The officer was in uniform at the time. Upon him were found a compass and small pieces of black bread and bacon, but no money. He was removed back to camp in the charge of an escort. Lane had escaped once before in this country and was then captured at Whitby.

Chapter Eight

German Submarine Officers

In early March of 1915, the British government took the decision to treat captured U-Boat officers and commanders, but not the ordinary crew members, more harshly than other captured German military personnel. These German officer submariners were no longer to be placed in internment camps with their peers, but instead in British jails, many in solitary confinement. This decision was a reaction to the highly successful 'unrestricted' U-Boat attacks upon British and Allied shipping, with the British press having for some time referred to German U-Boat officers and men as 'pirates'. There were even calls in some quarters for these 'pirates', when taken prisoner, to be 'summarily hanged'!

Since the outset of the war, the British had been sending many 'dangerous U-Boat pirates' to Dyffryn Aled, where they were nicely out of the way. Once the German authorities got wind of Britain's new policy, the German government removed several British officers from 'normal' internment camps and placed them in detention barracks. Some records give the number as thirty-seven, while others list thirty-nine. In addition, the British had given the Germans something of a propaganda coup. Via the press, the German authorities expressed outrage, mainly for the consumption of then neutral countries, particularly the United States.

The *Dundee Courier* of Monday, 12 April 1915 had this on the matter:

GERMANY'S LATEST THREATS
BRITISH PRISONERS TO SUFFER FOR
'SHAMELESS' TREATMENT OF CAPTURED
SUBMARINE CREWS
Amsterdam, Sunday

Commenting on the announcement by the British Government that special treatment was reserved for German submarine prisoners, the Kreuz Zeitung says:

'If the officers and crews of our submarines are placed in such institutions [naval detention barracks] then this is a shameless and degrading procedure for which British prisoners in our hands will suffer severely.

'The Hamburger Nachrichten publishes a violent leading article on the subject of reprisals, in the course of which it says enemy soldiers captured by us are treated with the greatest consideration. We must now recognise how matters stand. We too must have the canals cleared (a reference to the work which it is alleged German prisoners are put in France). We must create prisons like those of the British Navy. As a punishment for the enemy that used them, dum-dum bullets must also whistle from German rifle barrels, and all the horrors that threaten German soldiers in the enemy's power must also exist for the sons of hostile nations.

'Letters which reach us ask why must our submarines always first hail British vessels, search them, and then tow the boats with their crews to safety. We know the British intend to be franc-tireurs on the sea. Otto Weddigen, with his loyal crew, have gone down like heroes, whom we mourn, and their loss cannot be compensated by the saving of British lives. Our enemies hope to conquer and know that victory justifies every method of warfare, even the most infamous. It therefore is a question of self-preservation for us to conquer. The lives of our warriors and the lives of Germans should be *our sole consideration, and for every act of harshness practised on Germans, manifold expiation should be exacted. The great numbers of prisoners which our armies have taken provides a means for the purpose. Humanity in the conduct of war at the cost of our own people is suicide.'*

James W. Gerard, the United States Ambassador in Berlin for four years until the United States relinquished their neutrality, wrote this in his *My Four Years in Germany – Memoir*:

While Winston Churchill was at the head of the British Admiralty, it was stated that the German Submarine prisoners would not be treated as ordinary prisoners of war; but would be put in a place by themselves on the grounds that they were pirates and murderers; and not entitled to the treatment accorded in general to prisoners of war. Great indignation was excited by this in Germany; the German government immediately seized thirty-seven officers, picking those they supposed were related to the most prominent families in Great Britain, and placed them in solitary confinement. A few were confined in this way in Cologne, but the majority were put in the ordinary jails of Magdeburg and Burg.

James W. Gerard and other United States officials made strong representations to the German authorities and managed to make visits to some of the 'British officer prisoners of war given special treatment by their German captors'.

The following is from the May 1915 entry in Daisy, Princess of Pless' self-titled book, *Daisy, Princess of Pless, by Herself*:

Winston Churchill's policy, I think it was his, of putting captured U-boat officers in jail in solitary confinement instead of treating them as ordinary prisoners-of-war, was, as I admitted to the Emperor, quite barbarous. It had naturally the most unfortunate results for British prisoners-of-war in Germany.

'The Emperor' mentioned in the above extract was Emperor Wilhelm II, who was the de-facto head of Germany during the First World War. Daisy, Princess of Pless (in German: *Furstin von Pless*), was born in 1873 at Ruthin, Denbighshire, North Wales. Her birthname was Mary Theresa Olivia Cornwallis-West, and she was the daughter of William Cornwallis-West, a British politician and wealthy landowner; and Mary 'Patsy' Adelaide Virginia Thomasina Eupatoria Cornwallis-West (nee Fitzpatrick), who was famous for her beauty, and for being a Victorian 'It Girl'.

In 1891, an eighteen-year-old Daisy had married Hans Heinrich XV, Prince of Pless, a wealthy German aristocrat of the Silesian nobility in the German Empire. Daisy resided in the Pless family property and became unhappy with her marriage and of living in Silesia, at the time part of the recently formed Germany. In August of 1914, with the outbreak of the First World War, things got more complicated for her. She longed to receive news from her homeland but was not allowed to mention Britain.

On 20 April 1915, Ivan Hay, a British officer POW in German hands who had been corresponding with Daisy, wrote this to her from his prison cell in Burg, Germany:

Do write as often as you can as I am all by myself in a jail: as the British Government has put all the German submarine people in jail, so the Prussian Government has put a corresponding number of us in prison. If you have got one or two English books you don't want I wish you would lend them to me. If you send anything down to the Gefangenen-lager they will send it on down here.

The *Birmingham Daily Mail* of Monday, 14 June 1915 had the piece below. It makes mention of Dyffryn Aled and references the British authorities having second thoughts as to the 'special harsher treatment' of captured German officer submariners:

CAPTURED PIRATES
BRITISH AND GERMAN RETALIATORY MEASURES
REQUEST TO AMERICA
(Official Press Bureau Message)

The Press Bureau on Saturday night issued the following:
'The following note has been addressed to his Excellency the American Ambassador by the Secretary of State for Foreign Affairs:
'The Secretary of State for Foreign Affairs presents his compliments to the United States Ambassador and has the honour to state that His Majesty's Government having decided to release from naval custody those naval prisoners of war who were saved from the submarines U8, U12 and U14, and to transfer them to the custody of the military authorities, to be confined under precisely the same conditions as other prisoners of war. Instructions having been given for the officers to be moved to Dyffryn Aled, Donington Hall, Holyport, and for the men to be interned in Shrewsbury, Frith Hall and Dorchester detention camps.

'His Majesty's Government expect that, in accordance with the undertaking of the German Government, they will at once send the thirty-nine British officers now under barrack arrest back to the ordinary detention camps, and

they will be glad to learn as soon as possible to which camps the officers in question have been sent and which officers have been sent to which camps.

'The Secretary of State will be much obliged if Mr Page will communicate the foregoing to the United States Ambassador at Berlin by telegram, and request Mr Gerard to obtain a reply from the German Government in regard to the matter at his earliest convenience – Foreign Office, June 12.'

The *Denbighshire Free Press* of Saturday, 19 June 1915 had information of new arrivals at Dyffryn Aled, and is without doubt directly related to the previous story:

SUBMARINE PRISONERS

During the week, several German Naval prisoners captured from German submarines have been brought to Dyffryn Aled Internment Camp.

The *Birmingham Daily Post* of Saturday, 26 June 1915 reported upon the ending of the retaliatory action by the German authorities:

BRITISH OFFICER PRISONERS.
RETURNED TO FORMER PLACES OF DETENTION

The Press Bureau says the United States Ambassador has communicated to the Foreign Secretary a telegram from the United States Embassy at Berlin, stating that all the thirty-nine British officers were returned to their former places of detention last week. Except for Lieutenant Goschen, who remains at the Lazaret, Magdeburg.

James W. Gerard, the United States Ambassador to Berlin, also wrote the following in his *My Four Years in Germany – Memoir*:

After Churchill left the British Admiralty [following the debacle of the Battle of Gallipoli] his successor reversed his ruling and the submarine prisoners were placed in the ordinary confinement of prisoners of war. When the Germans were assured of this, the thirty-seven British officers who had in reprisal been placed in solitary confinement, were sent back to what were called 'good camps'.

Chapter Nine

Everyday Matters

Sporting activities and religious services

Dyffryn Aled had a sports field, a flat meadow area devoid of trees and separated from the mansion by the River Aled (in Welsh: *Afon Aled*). This sports field was not fenced, as the German officer POWs were placed on the gentlemanly notion of 'parole', having given their word not to escape while taking part in sporting activities. It was thought that physical activities might help to relieve the boredom of their internment, and every second or third day they were permitted to go on accompanied (by guards) walks, again having given their parole not to try to escape.

Religious services were held regularly at Dyffryn Aled for the German officer POWs, as well as for the British soldiers who guarded them. Several temporary hutments were erected on the perimeter of the mansion itself. These huts included a hospital hut, officers' quarters, and administrative

GERMAN PRISONERS PLAYING ON THE DYFFRYN ALED FIELD

Dyffryn Aled POW camp

huts. In addition, a number served as quarters for the soldiers stationed there.

It is interesting to contrast the daily life of POWs at Dyffryn Aled with an entry in Daisy, Princess of Pless, by Herself. In the book, a German officer who was interned there is mentioned by name in a correspondence from Tuesday, 1 December 1914, recounted on pages 307 to 308:

On December 1, Countess Brockdorff, Mistress of the Robes to the Empress, wrote urging me to try to communicate with a relation of hers, Lieutenant Hans Werner von Helldorff, who was a prisoner-of-war at Abergele, in Denbighshire. It is near Rhyl and Ruthin. I must quote some of Countess Brockdorff's letter just to show what a close friend of the Empress was at this time being told about the way German prisoners were treated in England:

DEAR PRINCESS,

You have got his address and wished to help him on. Please do not postpone your letter; he is ill, suffering from kidney, liver and bile – for want of air and exercise. The prisoners are allowed to walk in a place fifty metres long and width. A short time you seemed not to think that there was cause to complain that eight officers are together in one room with only three chairs and three washing stands – for so long! Please add to this, the fact that they had often mould bread, meat already putrefied – too bad! Eighty-four officers in one house; the other night there was a fire on the roof and the hundred and forty men in the house – with one small staircase – seemed to have been in real danger.

But that could not be helped; but really the treatment they have to go through is a shame. And this poor Helldorff writes to his sister, Frau von Plessen, and to his other sister, who is my niece, that he wished to be dead. Don't you think

*they could allow him a cure somewhere being actually a
sufferer and ill? He must have some treatment, better food
and exercise. He has written seventeen letters, only four
arrived here. Please, my dear Princess, do write for him. I
fear you ought to try and write in German to a neutral, and
let it be translated into English, so that it may pass from
Germany to England. It is all so sad.*

*Yours very sincerely,
W. Brockdorff.*

While Lieutenant Hans Werner von Helldorff may well have
been unwell, and it was true that a fire had occurred at
Dyffryn Aled, he was most certainly telling 'porky pies' in his
letters back to Germany. His description of life and more
particularly the food provided were lies – false propaganda
which would then be passed on by his two sisters!

German officers in the First World War, especially
Prussian ones, felt they were the elite. Unlike their British
counterparts, they did not go out on patrols into no-mans-
land, and instead left such matters to their NCOs and their
men. While many British officers were somewhat aloof from
the men under their command, they did share a great deal of
their risks.

An account of the life of 'relative luxury' for German
officer POWs at Dyffryn Aled appeared in the *Manchester
Courier and Lancashire General Advertiser* of Thursday, 26
November 1914:

OFFICER'S LUXURIES

*Ninety-five German officers are interned at Dyffryn Aled,
Denbighshire. It is some ten miles distant from the nearest
railway station and the place is to be reached only by a
toilsome journey over a mountainous district.*

Otherwise, it would be difficult to better the conditions under which these gentlemen from the Kaiser's commissioned ranks are living, and this much is not disputed. If allowance be made for the limitations necessarily imposed by the loss of liberty, Dyffryn Aled at the present time would forcibly remind any observant visitor of a house party at a country mansion. The officers have with them 30 servants and a chef. There is a mess president and a mess secretary. With the last named I had some conversation. One does not meet every day an official, with such a flow of animal spirits, or one displaying such boisterous good humour. The menu submitted by him to the Commandant is his daily care. Being a German, he knows what German tastes are and he does his best to meet them. He secures an 'English breakfast, a German luncheon and an English dinner'. He had not yet reached the limit of what is possible, but 'the cuisine is excellent'. He volunteered this testimony quite freely.

The daily life, is of course, uneventful. Music and the usual card games are provided. The more studiously inclined pass a portion of their time reading and others who have been more accustomed to the gloves, make boxing their

Two German Officers POW's in a room at Dyffryn Aled

principal sport. Newspapers are forbidden in this and in all the camps.

A detailed account of Dyffryn Aled, and of the visit by the *Daily Mail*'s special correspondent to the camp in December 1914, appeared in New Zealand's *Marlborough Express* of Friday, 15 January 1915:

The building is a rambling old mansion, where ninety-eight German officers and thirty-seven soldiers and civilians are held as prisoners. The spacious rooms are embellished with wood carvings and ceilings by Adam. There is an exercise field of three acres. The prisoners receive half the pay of their rank, calculated by British infantry, which is 5s 9d in the case of Oberleutnant von Tirpitz, who has the rank of Captain. They are permitted to conduct their mess on identical lines with that of a British infantry battalion, with the privilege of electing a mess president, a secretary, and committees.

They are at liberty to drink lager beer, light wines, red and white, cognac, and mineral waters. The discretion of the commandant is practically never exercised. They smoke cigars, pipes, and cigarettes at will, and are supplied with a piano and other facilities for music. They are allowed to maintain their own library and to embellish their quarters with pictures of the Kaiser. They have the alternative of wearing German uniform or civilian attire as they please, and are allowed to employ the service of English tailors, haberdashers, and boot makers. Their fellow-prisoners act as the servants of the officers and also receive pay.

The prisoners have the right of presenting to the commandant every morning a list of wishes and requirements. These are freely granted almost without exception. The correspondent, arriving just before luncheon, visited the kitchen, presided over by a former chef of the Imperial Hotel at Torquay, a detained German Alsatian, who was found with sketches and memoranda. The daily fare is as follows:

Breakfast: Coffee, bacon, sausage, jam, bread and butter, and porridge. Lunch: Soup, a joint of beef, mutton or veal, vegetables and fruit. Dinner: A joint or cold meats, fried potatoes, soup, warm vegetables, cheese, and tea or coffee.

Dinner is served at 4.30 in the afternoon. The men sleep four, six, or eight in a room, according to the size of the room. From immediately after breakfast, at 8.30, the men are at liberty to remain in the open until dusk. The compound is surrounded by barbed wire, with sentries stationed at certain points. A new building has been erected as an infirmary, but so far has had no patients.

In early 1915, stories had appeared in the British newspapers that German POWs at internment camps in Britain were 'living a luxurious life in fine palatial surroundings'. To counteract these allegations, a deputation from the House of Commons visited a number of camps, including Dyffryn Aled and Donington Hall. This is an extract taken from their report on Dyffryn Aled.

Dyffryn Aled Officer's Camp in North Wales is described as an inaccessible, gloomy, mildewed-looking house, with all the windows on the front side covered with iron bars. It was previously used as a private lunatic asylum. The kitchen seemed about the best room in the house… There are no fixed baths, but the officers' valets carry hot water from the kitchen for hip baths. As regards the site of Dyffryn Aled, it is only fair to quote the U.S. report: 'The situation of the house in a romantic valley among the Welsh mountains is fine and healthy.'

Female visitors for German POWs!
The *Western Gazette*, amongst several newspapers, had this story in their Friday, 23 April 1915 edition:

GERMANS' FEMALE VISITORS
SOCIAL DINNER PARTIES IN THE CAMPS IN BRITAIN

It is understood that the attention of the authorities will be called this week in the House of Commons to the readiness with which commandants of camps where German prisoners are interned, are getting passes for the benefit of would-be visitors.

It is felt that the issue of these passes, which turns the camp into a species of social centre, is bad enough in any case, but it is rendered a good deal worse by the fact that a number of the persons availing themselves of these facilities are females who call more especially on officers with whom they have a chance acquaintance.

Unless some action is taken there is a risk of a certain amount of ill-considered female 'hero-worship', which would be the more objectionable in view of the treatment meted out to our officers and men in Germany.

In some of the camps it is even not uncommon for social dinner parties to be given.

This matter of German officer POWs in Britain receiving visits from females who were not in any way related to the captives, was discussed in the House of Commons:

House of Commons Written Answers on 27th April 1915
German Officers Interned

Question by Sir W. Bull: 'Asking the Under-Secretary of State for War as to how many passes for male visitors and how many for female visitors were issued by the respective Commandants of the various camps for Interned German

Officers in this country from 1st January to 19th April.'

Mr Tennant replied: 'At Holyport, 34 passes for males and 35 for females; at Bevois Mount, 6 and 10; Donington Hall, 4 and 4, and Dyffryn Aled, 5 and 7.'

An official visit to Dyffryn Aled

The American lawyer, Boylston Adams Beal, special attache' to the German Division of the United States Embassy in London, made an official visit to Dyffryn Aled to check on conditions there. Below is an account which appeared in the *Birmingham Daily Post* on Thursday, 14 September 1916. It should be remembered that the United States was still following its rather 'rocky' path of neutrality at this point in the conflict:

DYFFRYN ALED

In the internment camp at Dyffryn Aled, a gentleman's country house, at Abergele, Mr Beal found 81 German prisoners – 16 military officers and 25 military servants; 36 naval officers and 1 naval servant, and 3 civil servants.

'In this camp', says Mr Beal, 'there was an amusement committee, a wine committee, a canteen committee, a house committee, a cigar and cigarette committee, and a postmaster-general. All these committees are chosen quarterly by the interned officers, who have absolute control over the management of the house – the only thing done by the British staff being to pay the monthly bills. The interned officers occupy their time by reading and study, inlaid work, carpentry and carpentering. They give much time to the study of languages, particularly Spanish. The officers asked that they might be allowed to take walks, under escort, in the surrounding country and that religious services should be held more often at the camp. Both matters were promised consideration.'

Mr Beal adds: 'Everything about this camp was found in excellent condition. The interned officers looked in good health and seemed contented. They have ample opportunity for exercise and the situation of the house, in a romantic valley among the Welsh mountains, is fine and healthy. There is no need for cells at this camp.'

Guarding the Dyffryn Aled POWs

One of the senior British officers in charge of guarding POWs at Dyffryn Aled was Captain William Twigge Ellis, born 1867, and originally of Bethesda, Caernarfonshire. A solicitor, he set up his own practice in Llanrwst, moving there with his Talysarn-born wife Jane (nee Evans) and seven Bethesda-born children. When the First World War arrived, the three eldest of his six sons volunteered for military service in the British Army. William Twigge Ellis, aged forty-eight, was commissioned himself on 14 March 1915, as a lieutenant in the 5th (Flintshire) Battalion, the Royal Welch Fusiliers. Due to his age and perhaps other factors, he was ensured home service, while his sons were overseas, on the frontline.

In early 1918, William Twigge Ellis was promoted to the rank of Captain in the 324th Protection Company of the Royal Defence Corps, and posted to Dyffryn Aled to guard the German officer POWs there. The Royal Defence Corps had been formed in March 1916, and was composed of men considered either too old or medically unfit for frontline duties. It was created to provide soldiers for security and guard duties inside the United Kingdom, thereby freeing younger, fitter men to go to fight. In addition to guarding POWs, they also guarded strategic locations such as ports and important bridges.

On the 1911 Census, William Twigge Ellis had written that of the nine children born to him and his wife, two had already died. Sadly, of their three sons who went to war, two were killed in action and one was seriously maimed, losing an arm. It is difficult to contemplate what the father's thoughts were while guarding the German POWs at Dyffryn Aled.

William Twigge Ellis died in December 1920, aged fifty-three.

A harsh winter and rationing

The winter of 1917/1918 was a rather harsh one in the higher parts of North Wales, especially where Dyffryn Aled was situated. The following is an extract taken from a piece which appeared in the *North Wales Chronicle* of Friday, 21 December 1917:

> *Snowbound roads in the Vale of Clwyd. Farmers unable to move stock. Gales and a heavy fall of snow, a few inches deep on the lower regions of the Vale, such as from Denbigh towards Rhyl.*
>
> *However, on Monday morning in the Llansannan and Llanefydd districts, around Henllan and around Ruthin, Llanelidan and Derwen, and the Bryneglwys areas, the snow was several feet deep.*
>
> *Farmers unable to get out around Llansannan. The Dyffryn Aled Camp was almost completely isolated. The men of the Transport Department having to dig their way along the roads to Denbigh.*

The civilian population of Britain, many of whom had relatives held in POW camps in Germany, were constantly seeking assurances from the British military and civilian authorities that German POWs in Britain were not receiving better food rations than they were. These concerns increased as the war relentlessly rolled on, thanks in large part to the German U-Boats having decimated merchant shipping. This article on the matter appeared in the *Denbighshire Free Press* newspaper of Sunday, 3 March 1918:

GERMAN PRISONERS' RATIONS

It is officially announced that the daily ration for prisoners of war, including of course the German prisoners of war at Dyffryn Aled Camp, Llansannan, will be as follows: Bread, 5 ozs; biscuits, 4 ozs; meat, 4 ozs on five days a week; herrings, 12 ozs on two days a week; tea or coffee, half ounce; sugar, 1 oz; jam, 1 oz; potatoes, 20 ozs; vegetables or fruit, 4 ozs; salt, quarter ounce; and oatmeal, 2 ozs weekly.

There has naturally been a good deal of local feeling as to the abundant supplies taken up to the Llansannan Camp, where the prisoners were said to be, 'living on the fat of the land', whilst local civilians were unable to get sufficient of the most necessary articles.

The rationing therefore has come none too early and will help to mitigate this local feeling, as whilst being ample for those interned, will bring them more into fair comparison with the civilian population.

The Under-Secretary of War in Parliament stated on Monday that the civilian population were free to purchase substitutes, whereas prisoners of war were restricted and the diet was the minimum prescribed by the medical authorities.

One of the regular providers of supplies for Dyffryn Aled was a very local source indeed. Elwyn Williams, formerly of Pandy, Bryn-Rhyd-Yr-Arian ('Bryn' to locals), and now of Abergele, remembers his late mother having spoken about Dyffryn Aled. As a young woman living in the village, she used to help at the local shop, *Siop y Bryn*. She would, a few times a week, travel up to Dyffryn Aled in a pony and trap, taking locally made bread and other provisions for the camp's 'guests' and guards.

The Saturday, 6 July 1918 edition of the *Derby Daily Telegraph* gave an account of proceedings in the House of Commons that related to the status of Wolfgang von

Tirpitz, as well as the rations enjoyed by German officer POWs in Britain:

GERMAN OFFICER PRISONERS
WHAT THEY ARE ALLOWED TO PURCHASE

Mr Macpherson, in a written answer to Colonel Faber, says that von Tirpitz was released for internment in Holland on January 9, in strict conformity with The Hague Agreement of 1917. He was captured in the North Sea on August 28th 1914 and was interned in the prisoner of war camp at Redford on August 30th. In September of that year he was transferred to the camp at Dyffryn Aled, where he remained until December last, when he was removed to Kegworth.

Officer prisoners of war in this country do not draw rations, but are allowed to purchase foodstuffs within certain limits which have been fixed by the War Office, with the approval of the Ministry of Food. The amount of meat purchased weekly must not exceed 16oz. of fresh meat (including bone) and 4oz. of preserved meat. 'As regards British officer prisoners of war in Germany I regret that there is no detailed information, but I fear that, as in the case of the men, the food conditions leave much to be desired', concludes Mr Macpherson.

'Rule, Britannia!'

Berwyn Evans, the respected local historian from Llansannan, Conwy, once spoke with me about Dyffryn Aled in the First World War. From him, I learnt of an amusing and quite charming story he had picked up from the late Mary Evans of Trelogan, Flintshire:

Mary Evans' elderly mother often reminisced about her childhood in Plas Isaf, Bryn-Rhyd-Yr-Arian ('Bryn'). During the summer holidays, she and the other village children would play around the River Aled and its old humpback, stone bridge. Half-a-mile away from the village, in the direction of Llansannan, Conwy, was Dyffryn Aled. Once a week, a lorry would pass through tranquil 'Bryn' on its way to deliver beer to the public houses of Llansannan. Because the main road was in such a poor state of repair, the driver had obtained permission to use the private estate road of Dyffryn Aled.

During one of the wartime summer holidays, Mary Evans' mother and her friends had chatted with the lorry driver and asked him if he would give them a ride on the back of his lorry the following week. The driver agreed, but with the condition the children learnt the first verse of the patriotic British song 'Rule, Britannia!'. These children barely spoke English between them, Welsh being very much their first language, but when the driver stopped in 'Bryn' a week later, he found they knew the words. The children jumped on board the lorry and off they went. Approaching Dyffryn Aled, the driver tuned to the children and said, 'Now sing "Rule, Britannia" as loud as you can!', which they did. One hour later, on the return journey, they were asked to do the same again.

'Rule, Britannia! is an old British song which emanated from the poem 'Rule, Britannia' by James Thomson. It was set to music in 1740 by Thomas Arne. Though this song is associated with the British Army, it is more strongly associated with the Royal Navy. 'Rule, Britannia!', the song, consists of six verses, the chorus of which is repeated:

Rule, Britannia!, Britannia, rule the waves
Britons never, never, never shall be slaves

There are slight variations on the exact wording of the song, including only singing the word 'never' once.

Chapter Ten

How Dyffryn Aled Gained its Guests

From the National Archives

The list below is of fifty-one German officers and high-ranking civilians interned at Dyffryn Aled. It was taken from the National Archives, Record Reference: FO 383/150. I have added to its content by my own research, and I have made some corrections. It is but a snapshot of those who were interned at Dyffryn Aled between the first week of September 1914 and late December 1918.

Officer	Rank	Vessel/Regiment
Oswald Arthur Robert ARNDT	Ober Ingenieur	Unknown U-Boat
Hans BEYER	Oberleutnant zur See	U-Boat 6
Karl Eduard Albert BIERMANN	Korvetten kapitan	Konigin Luise
Heinrich Albert BOTHMANN	Kfw. Officer	Konigin Luise
Friedrich BRAUNE	Oberleutnant zur See	V.187
Iwan CROMPTON	Oberleutnant zur See	U-Boat 41
Friedrich Edward Carl DETLEFSEN	Leutnant	Konigin Luise
Christian Julius Gustave ECKENBRECHT	Oberleutnan	Reserve Infantry. Reg.242
Gerhardt FURBRINGER	Kapitanleutnant	U-Boat 40
Reinhold GADOW	Kapitanleutnant	Konigin Luise
Ernst GRAEFF	Kapitanleutnant	U-Boat 36
Wilhelm Hermann GROSS	Marine Ingenieur	U-Boat 23
Constantin Friedrich Carl HARTE	Hauptmann	Infantry Regiment 77
Max Gustave Theodor HEINISCH	Leutnant	Res. Inf. Reg.242, Kp.8

Hans Werner von HELLDORFF	*Leutnant*	*Garde du Corps*
Georg Heinrich Julius von HENNIG	*Kapitanleutnant*	*U-Boat 18*
Johannes Heinrich JOHANNSEN	*Ober Ingenieur*	*SMS Mainz*
Wilhelm KORRENG	*Leutnant Ingenieur*	
Egon Horst Alfred von KOSCHUTZKI	*Leutnant*	*Leib. Kur.Regiment 1*
Ernst Otto Wilhelm LANDWEHR	*Hauptmann*	*Infantry Regiment 158*
Martin Carl Herm.Theo. LOEWENSTEIN	*Oberleutnant zur See*	*Unknown U-Boat*
Robert MANN	*Marine Ingenieur*	*U-Boat 14*
Erich MASKOW	*Marine Ingenieur*	*U-Boat 6*
Johann Ludwig MOSLE	*Hauptmann*	*Jag. Battalion 9*
Hans Wilhelm MUELLER	*Leutnant zur See*	*Unknown U-Boat*
Johnny Martin MUHLAU	*Kapitanleutnant*	*U-Boat 14*
Paul MULLER	*Oberleutnant*	*Ldwehr. Inf. Regiment 13*
Dr Paul Wolfgang MULLER	*Kriegsfriew*	*Automobil Corps*
Otto Karl Wilhelm NEUERBURG	*Leutnant zur See*	*U-Boat 18*
Fritz NEUMANN	*Oberleutnant zur See*	*U-Boat 23*
Hisso von PETERSDORF	*Leutnant*	*Garde Schutze Battalion*
Prince Ernst von RATIBOR und CORVEY	*Oberleutnant zur See*	*U-Boat 23*
Edward RADTKE	*Leutnant*	*Infantry Regiment 27*
Henry RAUSCH	*Rittmeister*	*Garde Kur*
Baron Ottomar von REDEN	*Leutnant*	*Ulan Regiment 13*
Ulrich RITTER	*Major*	
Willy ROHLFFS	*Marine Ingenieur*	*SMS Mainz*
Max RUPPERSBERG	*Leutnant zur See*	*U-Boat 14*

Wilhelm SCHATZLE	*Hauptmann*	*Infantry Regiment 27*
Hans SCHULTHESS	*Oberleutnant zur See*	*U-Boat 23*
Fritz George SPRENGER	*Marine Ober*	
	Ingenieur	*U-Boat 18*
Richard STOBBE	*Oberleutnant zur See*	*U-Boat 40*
Ernst STRAUMER	*Leutnant*	*Reserve Inf. Reg. 242*
Alfred SYMONS	*Oberleutnant*	*U-Boat 14*
Christian Theodore Oskar		
TAPPE	*Ober Ingenieur*	*Konigin Luise*
Egon TERKS	*Zahlmeister*	*SMS Mainz*
Hermann THOLENS	*Kapitanleutnant*	*SMS Mainz*
Wolfgang von TIRPITZ	*Oberleutnant zur See*	*SMS Mainz*
Wilhelm Hermann Ludwig		
Fried. WALLIS	*Korvettenkapitan*	*V.187*
Joachim Lorens Carl von		
WEDEL	*Oberleutnant zur See*	*SMS Mainz*
Paul WENNEKER	*Leutnant zur See*	*SMS Mainz*

Using the above, we'll explore the vessels from which some of the POWs at Dyffryn Aled were captured, as well as the men themselves.

SMS Mainz

From the *SMS Mainz*, a *Kolberg*-class light cruiser of the Imperial German Navy, there were seven officers who ended up as POWs at Dyffryn Aled, including the first officer Captain-Lieutenant Hermann Tholens.

The *SMS Mainz* was built in 1908 by the Aktien-Gesellschaft Vulcan (AG Vulcan) shipyard at Stettin, a major seaport. The ship was launched in January of 1909 and commissioned into Germany's burgeoning High Seas Fleet (*Deutschlands Hochseeflotte*) in October of that year. Her armaments consisted of 12.0-x-4.1-inch guns; 4.0-x-2.0-inch guns; and 2.0-x-17.7-inch torpedo tubes. She had a top speed of around twenty-six knots and was used as a reconnaissance ship following Britain's declaration of war on 4 August 1914.

It was on 28 August 1914 that the *SMS Mainz* was patrolling around Heligoland Bight. The British Royal Navy had been closely monitoring, via their submarines, the activities of German vessels in the vicinity, and it was decided to attack with destroyers and light cruisers from Harwich.

The British naval force left Harwich on 26 August 1914, encountering a German torpedo boat on the morning of 28 August 1914. This vessel quickly headed towards the relative safety of nearby German battle cruisers, and so began the Battle of Heligoland Bight.

The *Stettin* and *Frauenlob* engaged the British ships while the *SMS Mainz* was ordered to cut off their retreat. This was overconfidence on the part of the Imperial German Navy. At 12.30 p.m, the *SMS Mainz* encountered the British *HMS Arethusa* and several destroyers. After about fifteen minutes of engagement, three more British cruisers arrived on the scene and the SMS Mainz had no alternative but to try to escape. At 1.00 p.m., a shell hit and jammed her rudder. By 1.20 p.m., her guns were almost completely disabled, her aft and centre funnels had collapsed, and she was now something of a 'sitting duck'. A torpedo from the British destroyer *Lydiard* struck a serious hit on her port side, and the commander, Wilhelm Pasche, gave the order to abandon ship. Just as he and his navigation officer were leaving their position in the armoured conning tower, a shell hit and killed them both. By 1.35 p.m., without working engines and guns, the game was up for the *SMS Mainz*.

V.187

Like the *SMS Mainz*, the torpedo boat *V.187* was also built

Torpedo Boat Destroyer V.187

by AG Vulcan, and she was launched on 11 January 1911, with a top speed of thirty-three knots. In the early weeks of the First World War, the *V.187* was attached to the 1st torpedo boat flotilla, and was under the command of Corvette Captain Wilhelm Hermann Ludwig Friedrich Wallis, better known as 'Willi' Wallis.

During the initial engagement at the Battle of Heligoland Bight, as the Imperial German Navy destroyers fled, the *V.187* made an audacious move, for she turned at full speed and passed between the British vessels. With dense mist aiding her cause, she managed to avoid *HMS Fearless* and *HMS Arethusa*, but was soon spotted by *HMS Nottingham* and *HMS Lowestoft*, which shelled her with broadsides. The *V.187* sank at 10.00 a.m., the first 'serious' naval loss of the war for the Imperial German Navy. Twenty-four of her crew were rescued, including Corvette Captain Willi Wallis, while sixty-four others perished.

SMS Konigin Luise

The *SMS Konigin Luise* had been a German steam-powered ferry which operated between Hamburg and Holland. On 3 August 1914, she was requisitioned by the Imperial German Navy for use as an auxiliary minelayer. Once refitted, she possessed two revolver cannons and could carry up to two hundred mines at any one time. She was disguised in the

SMS Konigin Luise

livery colours of the British Great Eastern Railway, as its steamships regularly sailed between Harwich and the Hook of Holland.

On the evening of 4 August 1914, the day Britain had declared war on Germany, the disguised *SMS Konigin Luise*, commanded by Corvette Captain Karl Eduard Albert Biermann, set sail from Emden with orders to lay mines in British waters. While carrying out her mission, she caught the attention of passing British trawlers, who informed the *HMS Amphion* and several other British ships of her activity on the morning of 5 August 1914. At 10.25 a.m., having located the suspicious vessel, *HMS Lance* and *HMS Landrail* moved to investigate, causing her to flee. *HMS Lance* opened fire with the very first British shots of the First World War. When *HMS Amphion* also began firing, Corvette Captain Karl Biermann realised he and his crew had no choice but to abandon ship. Scuttled, the *Konigin Luise* soon rolled over to port and sank at about 12.20 p.m.

Forty-six of the *Konigin Luise*'s crew, including Corvette Captain Karl Biermann, were rescued and shared between the British ships present. Meanwhile, *HMS Amphion* sighted another ship, similar in shape and size to the *Konigin Luise*, though this one boldly flew a huge German flag. It was the *St Petersburg*, and some of the British naval force began firing upon it. *HMS Amphion's* officers realised this German ship was 'officially' carrying the German Ambassador from Britain back to Germany, and so she bravely manoeuvred herself between the British vessels and the *St Petersburg*, thereby avoiding a very serious 'diplomatic incident', one which could have swayed neutral countries towards the side of Germany.

In the early hours of 6 August 1914, *HMS Amphion* was returning to Harwich along the route she was ordered to, when at about 3.30 a.m., one of the mines laid by the *SMS Konigin Luise* struck her! The bridge was destroyed and smoke and flames engulfed her. Only one of the gun crew in the fo'c'sle survived, and those who were on the bridge, including the captain, were badly burnt. As it was breakfast time on the *HMS Amphion*, many of the crew were in the forward mess decks and were killed by fire or smoke inhalation. Those who died included nineteen of the twenty-one Germans who had been 'rescued' from off the *SMS Konigin Luise*!

HMS Amphion sank and was the first British naval loss of the war. A few weeks later, five of the rescued German officers from the *SMS Konigin Luise*, including its commander, were interned at Duffryn Aled.

U-Boat 6

The *U-6* was launched on 18 May 1910, being commissioned by the Imperial German Navy on 12 August 1910. The *U-6* underwent four separate patrols in wartime between 5 August 1914 and 15 September 1915. During these, she sank sixteen ships and took a further three ships as prizes.

U-Boat 6

The *Sheffield Evening Telegraph* of Wednesday, 11 April 1917 had an informative piece on the way the German's dealt with vessels captured as prizes during the war:

U-BOAT REWARDS

A correspondent of the 'Telegraaf' on the frontier says the Amsterdam correspondent of 'The Times' states that German submarine crews receive the same pay as those of other naval vessels, with the addition of 10 percent, and prize money.

In the case of captured ships, the commander and first engineer each receive 5 per cent of the ship's value as estimated by the Prize Court; the officers may share 15 per cent of the value; and the crew share 25 per cent between them. Thus 50 per cent of the value of captured ships goes to the submarine crews. The reward for torpedoed ships is smaller. The ship's assured value is here taken as the basis. The commander and the chief engineer both get 1 per cent; the officers 4 per cent together; and the crew 10 per cent together.

During the first six months, the reward paid to a submarine are somewhat higher. A special prize is given to commanders who destroy most warships on a voyage, and also for special feats.

The German Kaiser 'in league' with the devil – a WWI postcard

This paying of a financial bounty to German U-Boat crews was partly the reason that the British dubbed them 'U-Boat pirates'. However, the practice was most certainly not a German invention, for it had been in operation for many hundreds of years. British seafarers, such as Sir Francis Drake and Sir Walter Raleigh, had been particularly adept at it.

On 15 September 1915, the *U-6* was torpedoed by the British submarine *HM E16*, killing twenty-four of her crew. The five survivors included two Imperial German Navy officers, both of whom soon found themselves at Dyffryn Aled.

U-Boat 14

The *U-14* was launched on 11 July 1911 and commissioned on 24 April 1912. During its last patrol, which began on 31 May 1915, it sank two ships before being disabled by the British *Oceanic II* on 5 June 1915. Only one of its crew died, Sub-Lieutenant Max Hammerle. Of the twenty-seven survivors, four were interned at Dyffryn Aled.

U-Boat 18

The *U-18* was built at Kaiserliche werft Danzig and

launched on 25 April 1912, being commissioned on 17 November 1912. It was said to have been the first 'ship with hostile intentions' to enter British waters since Napoleonic times.

Going back to sea on 14 November 1914, the *U-18* left her moorings to patrol off the Orkney Islands. On 22 November, she was south of these when Captain-Lieutenant Georg Heinrich Julius von Hennig saw searchlights emanating from the direction of Scapa Flow, the natural harbour used by the British Navy. He believed that many of the British Grand Fleet would be at anchorage there, and made an 'executive decision' to enter 'the lion's den' to make an attack. At the opening to Scapa Flow, which he took for granted would be guarded, he was surprised to see the Pentland Skerries Lighthouse glaring. Unknown to him, it had been lit to enable an evacuation of the British fleet sometime before his arrival.

At about 11.00 a.m., with the assistance of a strong tide, the *U-18* tentatively edged into Scapa Flow. Captain-Lieutenant von Hennig and his crew were in luck, as the

German U-Boat, the U-18

protective boom-net to the anchorage that stretched from shore to shore was open for an expected British steamship to pass through. He raised the *U-18*'s periscope to look around the anchorage for targets, but the area was devoid of any ships of the British Grand Fleet.

At 11.20 a.m., the *U-18* manoeuvred around to head back into open sea, but the crew of the steamer *Tokio* spotted her periscope and quickly raised the alarm. A number of British ships began patrolling to find this audacious enemy U-Boat and her crew. The *U-18* made for Pentland Firth, but to do so had to sometimes travel at periscope-only depth. Her luck ran out when at 12.10 a.m she was spotted in the waters around Hoxa Head by Captain Youngson on the *Dorothy Gray*, a former fishing trawler now being used as an auxiliary minesweeper.

Captain Youngson made the decision to ram the enemy U-Boat and headed in the direction of her periscope. The *Dorothy Gray* hit the *U-18* with great force, so much so that the *Dorothy Gray* was said to have been raised three feet into the air. Her crew became very excited and started throwing anything heavy or jagged aboard their ship at the U-Boat. Captain-Lieutenant von Hennig thought quickly and ordered the U-Boat to make a desperate run for the safety of open water. The ramming had resulted in the *U-18*'s steering gear and hydroplanes being damaged, making control impossible. She was veering and struck the seabed, thrusting her straight back up. As the *U-18* hit the surface, she did so right in front of the *HMS Garry*, which had answered an excited radio message from the *Dorothy Gray*.

The *U-18* desperately crash-dived, but here the seabed was only some 230 feet down, and she hit it for the second time, damaging her front. Captain-Lieutenant von Hennig ordered the U-Boat to drive towards the open sea. After travelling a short distance, she hit a rock, causing her propellers to be damaged and a fire to break out in the battery room. Looking around at his crew, Captain-Lieutenant von Hennig ordered all the tanks to be blown, causing the badly damaged *U-18* to surface for the very last time. The white flag was taken from his cabin and the crew made their way up onto the exposed hull of their U-Boat. They raised the white flag and fired off a star shell.

U-Boat 23

The *U-23* was launched on 12 April 1912 and commissioned on 11 September 1913. During her patrols in the First World War, she had four different commanders. The fourth and last, from 13 January 1915 onwards, was Sub-Lieutenant Hans Schulthess.

By 20 July 1915, the *U-23* had sunk a total of seven ships. She was then torpedoed by the British submarine *HM C27*, working with the decoy British trawler, the *Princess Louise*. Twenty-four of the *U-23*'s crew were killed, while ten survived. Four of these were officers, and all were soon interned at Dyffryn Aled. These officers were Sub-Lieutenant Hans Schulthess; Sub-Lieutenant Ernst von

U-Boat U-23 at the Kiel Shipyards

Ratibor und Corvey; Sub-Lieutenant Fritz Neumann; and Marine Engineer (in German: *Marine Ingenieur*) Wilhelm Hermann Gross.

U-Boat 36
The *U-36* was launched on 6 June 1914 and commissioned on 14 November 1914. Under the command of Captain-Lieutenant Ernst Graeff the *U-36*, she went on two patrols, sinking fourteen ships, and taking three more as prizes.

On 24 July 1915, the *U-36* was sunk by gunfire from the British Q-Ship, *Prince Charles*. Eighteen of her crew were killed, but fifteen to sixteen were rescued. We can be sure about who one of these survivors was, as a few weeks later the *U-36*'s commander, Ernst Graeff, was at Dyffryn Aled.

U-Boat 40
The *U-40* was launched on 22 October 1914 and commissioned on 14 February 1915. She only went on one patrol and sank no ships. On 23 June 1915, she was torpedoed by the British submarine *HM C24*, assisted by the *Taranaki*, a decoy trawler. Of the *U-40*'s crew, twenty-nine were killed, with only three surviving. The three survivors were: Captain-Lieutenant Gerhardt Furbringer; Sub-Lieutenant Richard Stobbe; and Boatswain (in German: *Bootsmann*) Beizen.

The two officers, Captain-Lieutenant Gerhardt Furbringer and Sub-Lieutenant Richard Stobbe, were interned at Dyffryn Aled.

U-Boat 41, Iwan Crompton, and the 'Second *Baralong* Incident'
The *U-41* was (and still is) enmeshed in allegations and recriminations. She was launched on 10 October 1914 and commissioned on 1 February 1915. By 23 September 1915,

Ob.-Lt. z. S. Crompton
Phot. Berl. Ill.-Ges.

Leutnant zur See Iwan Crompton,
WWI

over the course of four patrols, she had sunk twenty-eight ships, taken one as a prize, and seriously damaged another.

On 24 September 1915, the *U-41* was the target of gunfire from the *Wyandra*, which had only recently reverted to its 'launch name' – earlier in this book, readers were introduced to her as the *'Baralong'*.

The commander of the *U-41* and thirty-four other crew members died, leaving only two survivors. One of these was Sub-Lieutenant Iwan Crompton, who despite his name was German born and bred. He was interned at Dyffryn Aled, but sometime in 1917, having lost one eye, was repatriated to Germany in an exchange deal of 'disabled officers'. Eventually, he published his full account of the *U-41*'s exploits, and more particularly serious allegations against the captain and crew of the *Baralong/Wyandra*.

What follows appear to be the salient facts in relation to the 'Second Baralong Incident': *U-41* was in the process of sinking the unarmed steamship *SS Urbino*, when the *Wyandra*, disguised as a neutral vessel by flying the flag of the United States, arrived at the scene. The *U-41*'s commander, Claus Hansen, ordered to surface close to the 'neutral ship' to check it out. As the submarine did so, the *Wyandra* opened fire on the *U-41* with quite devastating effect.

The United States were still officially neutral when *The New York Times* published, in their edition of Sunday, 5 November 1916, the German Admiralty account below:

The German Admiralty has furnished to The Associated Press correspondent the details of what is characterized as a 'Second Baralong Case', in which a British patrol ship flew American colours. It is declared after destroying the submarine U-41, it deliberately ran down a rowboat with only two survivors of the undersea boat in an endeavour to remove the only witnesses and has since prevented the intended victims, who were almost miraculously saved, from communicating the news to their own Government.

The incident, according to the German Admiralty occurred on Sept. 24, 1915 and has only just been learned of through an invalided prisoner transferred to Switzerland. The submarine according to the account, had halted in the neighbourhood of the Scilly Isles for examination of a steamer under the American flag, apparently an innocent merchantman. The steamer ostensibly prepared to lower a boat, but when the submarine had approached to within 300 yards, the supposed merchantman suddenly opened concealed ports and began firing from two cannons and also with rifles, the American flag flying the whole time. The account continues – the submarine irreparably damaged, went under, but was able to come to the surface later for an instant. Lieutenant Crompton, seriously wounded and Petty Officer Godau managing to crawl out through an open hatch before the submarine sank forever.

The sole survivors ultimately managed to swim to an empty boat. The steamer, observing this, according to the German Admiralty officials, headed full speed for the boat, not to save, but to ram it, placing a lookout in the steamer's bow to facilitate accurate steering. The Germans at the last moment sprang from the boat and clung to the wreckage of it for a half hour, when the steamer finally picked them up.

Lieutenant Crompton and his comrade were left without the slightest medical attention in a small cage on the steamer's deck until her arrival at Falmouth the following day. It is declared, although the Lieutenant had a double fracture of the jawbone, a broad wound across the nose and cheek, wounds in the left temple, and on the finger and an eye shot out. It was not until Sept. 29, that the Lieutenant was transferred to a shore hospital, clad at the time only in his underclothing, being transferred on Nov. 6 to the military prison in York Castle. Whence the wounded officer, whose wounds were still open and who was threatened with the loss of the other eye, was sent in mid-December to Dyffryn Aled, Wales, the account states. A British surgeon later proposed to transfer the wounded officer, as totally invalided, to Switzerland and a Swiss commission of surgeons twice voted that he be thus sent, but the British Surgeon General, it is declared, vetoed the plan and the officer was kept in England. The German Admiralty declares that this was evidently due to a guilty conscience on the part of the British, who wished to prevent the news being made known. Lieutenant Crompton repeatedly attempted to send his report through the American Embassy in London, it is asserted, but no report from him reached Germany.

A German Admiralty officer recalling the newspaper reports of some time ago, that the British Government, having been forced by German retaliatory measures to abandon drastic treatment of captives from submarines, had given orders to take no submarine prisoners but to send them to the bottom with their vessels, declared to the correspondent that this case, with that of the 'Baralong' should be considered as furnishing all necessary proof that the story regarding the Government order was true.

The Submarine U-41 was commanded by Lieutenant-Commander Hansen, accounted one of the bravest and best of German submarine officers. So far as is known no previous intimation has been given by the German Admiralty of the loss of the submarine U-41, nor has any report regarding her been made by the British authorities. Unofficially it has been stated in England that numbers of German submarines have been accounted for by British naval forces, but the usual British Admiralty policy has been to make no announcements in this connection.

But the British Admiralty did decide, on this occasion, to 'speak out publicly' with a full rebuttal of the German allegations over the 'Incident'. This rebuttal appeared in a number of British newspapers, including the *Exeter and Plymouth Gazette* of Tuesday, 7 November 1916:

'SECOND BARALONG CASE'
Pirates Allege British Brutality
Admiralty Statement.
U-41 and a Merchant Steamer
Rescue of Survivors
An Absolute Lie.
Typical German Mentalities

The Secretary of the Admiralty last night made the following announcement:
'The German Press are trying to make capital out of what they describe as a Second Baralong Case. One object may be conjectured to be the incitement of opinion against Great Britain: another the revision of the argument in favour of an 'Unrestricted Submarine Campaign'. The facts are perfectly simple. On the morning of the 24th September 1915 in the Western Channel, the U-41 was engaged in sinking

a British merchant steamer. While she was so engaged a converted merchant vessel, commissioned as one of His Majesty's auxiliary ships, approached the submarine and the sinking vessel. Her character was not at once recognised, and in order that the submarine might not submerge before she was in range, she hoisted neutral colours – a perfectly legitimate ruse de guerre. When in range she hoisted a white ensign, as all British ships of war are required to do, fired on and sank the submarine.

'The immediate preoccupation of her Commander was to rescue the crew of the British vessel sunk by the submarine, who had been compelled to take to their boats fifty miles from the nearest port. When this had been done, the HM Ship closed on one of the boats of the sunken steamer; which had broken adrift, into which two survivors of the submarine had climbed. These were rescued in the same way as, but after their victims. The use of a neutral flag in order to approach within range of an enemy is a recognised practice of Naval War, and has been repeatedly adopted by the Germans themselves in this war. The Moewe for instance secured most of her victims by this method.

'It is difficult to believe that anybody except a German, would, based on these facts make an accusation of 'brutality' on the ground that it was the English, and not the German survivors who were saved first by the matter of a few minutes. The whole allegation affords an edifying example of the typical German mentality. It is the first obligation of the non-German to save German life. No reciprocal obligation rests on the German. Any surprise or ruse de guerre by the Germans is legitimate. All become illegitimate when practised against Germans. The statement that the Admiralty had ever issued orders that survivors of German submarines need not be rescued is an absolute lie, and was explicitly denied in the "Note of the Government on the Baralong Case, dated the 25th February 1916".'

Sub-Lieutenant Iwan Crompton, having returned to Germany via Switzerland, was able to tell his own unexpurgated version of the sinking of the *U-41*. Unsurprisingly, his very anti-British account did not appear in British newspapers, but it did appear in many newspapers abroad, including New Zealand's *Oamaru Mail*, on Saturday, 31 March 1917:

Lieutenant Crompton's report reads:
'On the morning of September 24, the British steamer Urbino bound for England, was sunk by artillery fire about thirty miles south-east of the Scilly Islands. The crew had been allowed about half an hour. When the Urbino was listing heavily and burning, a smoke cloud was sighted. Submarine 41 submerged and let a steamer pass at a distance of about 200 yards. The steamer flew the American flag. It had no neutrality sign on the side.

'The submarine emerged and ordered the steamer to stop. This order was immediately obeyed and the two vessels approached each other at a slow speed. We signalled an order to send the documents on board. This was not answered by the steamer, which gave the counter signal, "I am stopping." At the same time the steamer prepared to lower a boat. On the submarine, the gun on the bow had been made ready.

'When the vessels were about 300 yards apart, the steamer suddenly opened a violent fire, first with rifles along the whole railing, then from 7.6 centimetre guns hidden behind the ship's side at the bow and stern. Although the commander had immediately ordered that the cannon on the bow be let alone, the sailors wanted to continue firing it and had to be brought away by the helmsman.

'The submarine had received several hits by shells shortly before the conning tower was submerged. During the entire

engagement, the steamer flew the American flag. To be sure, the flagstaff was turned down, but the flag was not replaced by the British one and continued flying.

'As we went under and the submarine went to the bottom, I was lying unconscious in the tower in consequence of a wound. When I returned to consciousness I was swimming. Neither the submarine nor the steamer was visible. After having swum for some time, I was passed by the steamer at a distance of about sixty yards. I called and raised my arms, but was sneered and spat at by the sailors. After a long time I saw an empty lifeboat of the steamer Urbino. When I had climbed into it I heard the helmsman calling for me and I took him in. In consequence of loss of blood, I was lying in the boat aft, while the helmsman sat at the bow.

'After some time, we saw the steamer again. We stood upright in the boat and waved our hands. The steamer changed her course and approached us at high speed. Soon we observed a man standing in the bow who directed the course of the boat and menaced us with his fist from time to time. As the steamer did not reduce her speed there was no doubt that she intended to ram us. Finally, they threw a rope and took us on board.

'Aside from the officers of the Urbino whom we recognised, nobody wore a uniform. The crew of the steamer, according to the declaration of the first mate, belonged to the Royal Naval Reserve, but all of them, including the officers, were clad as civilians. When we arrived on board we were led to the stern and had some brandy. As no surgeon was aboard the helmsman bandaged me as well as possible. Then we were locked in a box standing on the deck. The box was so low we could not sit upright. We did not get any warm clothing. On the deck was a mattress with two covers and a pillow. The box was closed with an iron barred door.

'On the morning of September 25, the steamer arrived at

Falmouth. A surgeon came on board and bandaged the British. The helmsman observed that ten hammocks with wounded and dead were taken off the steamer. At this time, I was taken out of the box but had no medical attention until the next day at noon. In the afternoon, the captain of the corvette, who spoke German perfectly, tried to interrogate me. I told him my name and in order to cut off all questioning regarding the submarine, declared that I had been unconscious when she went to the bottom. The British were perfectly informed about all naval affairs. They knew the names of many submarine commanders and knew even the date when Submarine 41 left her home port.

'I had been separated from the helmsman on the morning of the 25th. The helmsman was interrogated on the bridge after me. In spite of all efforts he did not succeed in ascertaining the name of the steamer. On September 26, I was taken on land and conveyed to a military hospital, being first lodged in a room with four British officers. The next day, by order of the captain of the port, I was lodged in barracks. I was temporarily tied in bed as I was suffering from violent cramps. A sentinel with a fixed bayonet constantly stood at my bed. For the rest the treatment was good. Surgeons and hospital attendants took care of me and were friendly.

'On the morning of October 6, I had to get up in order to be taken to a large hospital. I was put on board torpedo boat No. 17, which soon made for sea. At noon we arrived at Plymouth. Escorted by a drunken warrant officer and six sailors I was carried to the naval detention barracks at Devonport. This was the same prison where the crew of Submarine 12 had been interned. In spite of my affirmations that my clothes were not ragged I was compelled to take them off. Helmsman Godau had been in this prison since September 26.

'After repeated requests I obtained a bed. The rations

were those of convicts and I could not eat them in consequence of my broken jaw. The medical assistance was absolutely insufficient. When I complained of this to the commander of the penitentiary he told me that he himself was sorry for it, but he had explicit orders from the commander at Plymouth. At my request, the commander called three days later and remedied some little deficiencies. The helmsman in spite of all his protests remained for about four weeks in the penitentiary.

'As I was in danger of becoming blind in the right eye also, I was taken on October 11 to the military hospital at Devonport. The broken jaw was treated again and a foreign substance detected. On October 18, I was operated upon and a brass screw which had been driven in by a shell explosion was removed. At the place where the jaw was broken, from within and without serious abscesses had formed meanwhile. Several brass splinters were shortly afterward removed from my left eye, the last one in January 1916. The treatment was generally good, but frequently the attendants stole food. I was not allowed to write letters.

'On November 6, I was transported to the York military prison, where I again met the helmsman. The commander telegraphed the Admiralty asking for instructions and received in answer an order to give no information. In these circumstances complaints were useless. There was no surgeon in the prison. About once a week the commander called with an oculist, who gave me very little care. After eight days the wounds in my temple became inflamed again and my jaw again swelled up. As there was no surgeon the helmsman cut the wounds with a pocket knife. The wound in the temple had not healed to this time and continues suppurating.

'On January 18, 1916, I sent a report to the American Embassy in which I pointed out particularly that Submarine 41 was fired at by a steamer flying the American flag. I also described the destruction of the submarine and the treatment *of the survivors in prison. When in the middle of February, I received no answer, I reported again, but again received no answer. In March, a gentleman from the American Embassy arrived at Dyffryn Aled. When I asked him whether he had received my reports, he said he knew nothing about them, and supposed that my reports were still in the War Office, as all communications directed to the American Embassy must first pass through the War Office.*

'When at the end of May, a physician committee arrived at the camp at Dyffryn Aled, I was immediately accepted for internment in Switzerland. On June 10, a second examination took place at the officers' camp at Holyport. The committee, contrary to regulations, as far as I knew, was composed of five British and two Swiss physicians.'

Willi Wallis

Wilhelm 'Willi' Hermann Ludwig Friedrich Wallis, who had been the German flotilla leader on the *V.187* at the Battle of Heligoland Bight, was the senior German officer during his time at Dyffryn Aled, and it was he who would make representations to the commandant on behalf of himself and the other POWs.

Being 'senior German officer', he wrote many official and personal letters. In one, dated 14 October 1914, he made mention of the strict censorship that was applied to all outgoing letters from Dyffryn Aled. He also remarked that his treatment by British officers since his capture had been 'above reproach'.

A further letter of Wallis' was forwarded on 5 October 1915 by the United States Embassy in London to the British Foreign Office. In this letter, Wallis made a number of complaints with regard to Dyffryn Aled, and his perceived unsuitability of it for German officer POWs. These complaints included that the mansion was in a neglected state, needing a number of more modern fittings and facilities.

He wrote that the windows and doors allowed drafts, that the roof leaked in places, and that the chimneys and fireplaces gave problems with smoke. He also stated there was discontent among the German officer POWs about having to share rooms.

Hermann Tholens

Hermann Tholens was born on 19 May 1882 in Leer, Germany. He joined the Imperial German Navy in April of 1900, and at the outbreak of the First World War, he was a captain-lieutenant and second-in-command of the *SMS Mainz*. On 28 August 1914, at the Battle of Heligoland Bight, he was rescued from the sea and taken prisoner. Soon, he found himself at Dyffryn Aled, and after his valiant but ultimately unsuccessful attempt to escape Britain and return to the Fatherland by U-Boat, he spent the remainder of the First World War in internment. Whilst still interned, Tholens was promoted to the rank of corvette captain on 19 June 1918.

Post-First World War, Tholens joined the National Socialist Workers Party (NSDAP), led by Hitler. In

December 1935, he was appointed to the rank of general labour leader (in German: *generalarbeits fuhrer*) in the Reich Labour Service (in German: *Reichsarbeitsdienst*). This was a major organisation in Nazi Germany, one used to solve the unemployment problem. Their remit was to achieve results by the militarisation of the workforce and to indoctrinate German workers in Nazi ideology. On 21 December 1944, Hermann Tholens received

Hermann Tholens in his WW2 nazi uniform

the high Nazi award of *Ritterkreuz dr Kriegsverdienstkreuzes mit Schwertern*, a form of the Knight's Cross.

Hans Werner von Helldorff

Hans Werner von Helldorff was from the Prussian aristocracy, and at the outbreak of the First World War, a lieutenant in the prestigious German Garde du Corps, which were the personal bodyguard of the German Emperor. As part of the 1st Guards Cavalry Division, they helped form the German 2nd Army.

Lieutenant Hans Werner von Helldorff was taken prisoner by the British on the Western Front, and due to his social status was sent to Dyffryn Aled. Along with Hermann Tholens and Heinz von Hennig, he was one of the POWs who escaped in August 1915 and planned to secure passage back to Germany on the *U-38*. After the Armistice, he was repatriated to Germany in November 1918.

In late September 1940, during World War II, Hans Werner von Helldorff was appointed chief of staff to Lieutenant-Colonel (in German: *Oberstleutnant*) Rudolf Graf von Schmettow, the force commander occupying the Channel Islands. They were constantly receiving orders direct from Berlin to subjugate the civilian population, but to their credit, von Helldorff and von Schmettow were suspected (probably correctly) of failing to implement several strict diktats.

Georg Heinrich Julius von Hennig

Georg Heinrich Julius von Hennig, known as 'Heinz' was born on 10 May 1883 at Gut Dembrowalonka, West Prussia. He came from an aristocratic and influential family. His grandfather had been the president of the Prussian parliament (in German: *Landtag*), while his father had served as Royal District Commissioner in Ostrowo, Posen, Prussia.

Heinz Von Hennig

Heinz von Hennig served in the Imperial German Navy before the outbreak of the First World War, and this included service as watch officer on the U-Boat *SMU 11* from 1909 to 1911. On 1 August 1914, he was made captain-lieutenant and put in command of the *U-18*. On her third patrol of the war, the vessel audaciously entered the 'home' of the British Grand Fleet at Scapa Flow, intending to torpedo as many ships as possible, but they were out of luck, as none of the British fleet was there at the time.

After the *U-18* was scuttled, von Hennig found himself at Dyffryn Aled, and was one of the three German officers who nearly escaped back to Germany on the *U-38*. Eventually, he was repatriated to his homeland, and by his retirement in 1931 had reached the rank of rear admiral (in German: *konteradmiral*). He was recalled to naval service during the Second World War, retaining his rank of rear admiral, but now served in the War Navy. He died on 29 November 1947 at Kiel, Germany, aged sixty-four.

Reinhold Gadow

The first officer on the *SMS Konigin Luise* when it was attacked on 5 August 1914 was Captain-Lieutenant Reinhold Gadow. He survived and endured a period of captivity on British soil until he was interned in the Netherlands on 13 January 1918. Allowed to return to Germany on 6 September 1918, after the war he served in several positions in the Germany Navy. He then took positions in the Reich's Defence Ministry until his retirement on 30 June 1930. As a retired admiral of the Weimar Republic, he became a naval correspondent for the *Deutsche Allgemeine Zeitung*.

Reinhold Gadow

The *Racine-Journal Times* of Wisconsin, United States, in their edition of Wednesday, 5 February 1936, had a statement from ex-Rear Admiral Reinhold Gadow:

The fast battleship is coming. I predict that all the big navies will follow the example of France and Italy by building fast, powerful and possibly un-sinkable battleships in the future. The size, armour and armaments of battleships have already been decided in favour of the French and Italian types. By building two battleships each, of greatest fighting power, floating safety and speed, France and Italy have already forced the issue. In other words, the fast battleship is coming. In relation to England, they have been for a number of years supplied with fast strong battle cruisers and battleships. They were modernised at an expense of half the costs of new construction. The Rodney and Nelson will not have to fear any adversary for years. As regards cruisers, the new heavy type of 10,000 tons has gained the upper hand over all other types of cruisers.

The 'Rodney' and 'Nelson' referred to by Gadow were two British Nelson-class battleships of the inter-war period. During this interbellum period, they were 'state of the art'. As Gadow predicted in 1936, capital ships were changing and the Nazi's War Navy needed to keep up with other major naval forces, especially the British and the French. In

1940 and in 1941, respectively, Nazi Germany commissioned the truly massive battleships, the *Bismarck* and the *Tirpitz*. These Bismarck-class battleships, heavily armed and with a top speed of some thirty knots (35 mph), were the largest and heaviest ever built for Germany.

Once the Second World War began, Gadow was recalled to duty, initially being described as 'at the disposal of the War Navy'. From September 1940 until March 1945, he was in the position of Director of Libraries for the Nazi's High Command of the Armed Forces (in German: *Oberkommando der Wehrmacht*). During this time, he was promoted to the rank of rear admiral. The High Command of the Armed Forces co-ordinated the efforts of the Army, Navy and Air Force. They were a kind of conduit for translating Hitler's ideas into military orders. As the war progressed, the High Command of the Armed Forces found itself more and more being the de-facto command for western German forces. They were infamous for having issued many brutal decrees and orders against innocent civilians and POWs.

Post-Second World War, in the Autumn of 1946, Reinhold Gadow is said to have gone missing around Saschsenhausen KZ, Oranienburg, Germany, having been abducted by the Russians, who regarded him as a Nazi war criminal. Saschsenhausen KZ was a vile Nazi concentration camp used primarily for the extermination of their political prisoners. Gadow's exact fate is not known, but it is not difficult to guess what it was, and he was never seen or heard from again.

Prince Ernst von Ratibor und Corvey

Prinz (in English: Prince) Ernst von Ratibor und Corvey, a son of Prince Egon and Princess Leopoldine, was born at Ratibor in Silesia on 5 August 1891. The family owned vast estates in Central Europe, and in 1918 were thought to be the biggest landowners in Germany.

Prince Ernst was a sub-lieutenant on the *U-23*, under the wartime command of Hans Schulthess. On 20 July 1915, the *U-23* went to attack what they thought to be a lone British fishing trawler, but in fact she was the British decoy trawler, the *Princess Louise*, which had back-up! The British submarine, the *C27*, then torpedoed the *U-23*, killing twenty-four of her crew. Ten survivors were rescued by the British Royal Navy, including Prince Ernst von Ratibor und Corvey, who soon became a long-term prisoner of war at Dyffryn Aled, North Wales, which is a very long way from Silesia.

In the inter-war period, Prince Ernst, who was said to be very wealthy, was a great financial supporter of Hitler and the Nazi Party in Germany, and he socialised in their circles frequently. At one time, he was almost certainly a full member of the Nazi Party. In the book, *Blood and Banquets; A Berlin Diary 1930-38*, by Bella Fromm, there is a very interesting anecdote from the 1930s which involves Prince Ernst von Ratibor und Corvey, his daughters, and Hitler:

> *Upon the arrival of the immensely rich Prince Ratibor und Corvey and his two daughters, Hitler was again overwhelmed. The Princesses mother is a granddaughter of Pauline Metternich. Ratibor is one of the paying members of the party. The young Princesses reacted with a proper show of pleasure to his hand kissing and his piercing glance.*

Bella Fromm, born in 1890, was a newspaper reporter on Berlin's 'social scene' in the 1930s. She witnessed first-hand the rise of Hitler and the Nazis, mixing socially with high-ranking party members, foreign diplomats, and with Hitler himself. As a Jewish woman, she helped other Jewish people to escape Germany at a time when their lives were quickly becoming endangered by the rabid anti-Semitism that the Nazis encouraged and spread. Bella Fromm herself, in 1938, fled to the United States, and smuggled out of Germany her diary collection, which if the Nazi's had found them, would have caused her to be imprisoned or sent to one of the extermination camps.

Friedrich Braune

Friedrich Braune was born on 6 October 1889 in Fehrbellin, Brandenburg, Germany. He entered the Imperial German Navy as a sea cadet, and from 3 April 1907 until 31 March 1908 underwent his basic training on board the *Stein*. Braune received promotion to acting sub-lieutenant on 28 July 1910, and to sub-lieutenant on 27 September 1913. From November 1912 to July 1914, he served on the torpedo boat S.138. With war looming, he was transferred to the *V.187* on 31 July 1914.

On 28 August 1914, Braune was on-board the *V.187* when it took part in the Battle of Heligoland Bight. Acting Sub-Lieutenant Jasper, also on-board the *V.187* at this time, gave a full account of the demise of the ship. Below is an extract taken from this:

I jumped overboard; just according to my calculations, the charges would take effect. The rest of the gun crew of the aft gun, which had continued firing to the last, among them was Leutnant Braune, sprang simultaneously into the water… I then hauled another sixteen survivors into my English boat. Another English boat under the command of an English officer was left behind by the destroyers in the evening. It had on board Leutnant Braune and several other survivors.

Acting Sub-Lieutenant Friedrich Braune was taken prisoner by the British Royal Navy and found himself at Dyffryn Aled. He spent a long period there until he was sent to the Netherlands for a 'kinder' form of internment.

Friedrich Braune in his WW2 uniform

Post-First World War, on 17 May 1919, he was promoted to the rank of captain-lieutenant, and then to corvette captain on 1 April 1926. He received a number of further inter-war promotions, until he was made rear admiral during the Second World War on 1 January 1941. At this point he became Senior Director of the War Navy's shipyard in Bergen, Norway, which was under German (Nazi) occupation.

Between 28 December 1939 and 30 March 1941, Rear Admiral Friedrich Braune served Nazi Germany as an officer-judge at the Reichs War Court, and did so again between 15 June and 31 July 1942. Braune then officially retired from the War Navy on 31 July 1942, to serve as a judge at the Prize Court in Berlin. A retired Rear Admiral, Friedrich Braune died in Flensburg, Schleswig-Holstein, Germany, on 29 June 1971, aged eighty-one.

Chapter Eleven

Following the Armistice

The *Cambrian Daily Leader* newspaper of Monday, 21 October 1918 had this:

PRISONERS OF WAR

Under the agreement between British and German Governments with regard to prisoners of war, the latter make it a stipulation to agreeing to remove British prisoners from certain camps that German officer prisoners should be removed from Dyffryn Aled to other officers' camps.

The Armistice finally arrived on 11 November 1918, and Dyffryn Aled was quickly wound down from being on a war footing, to being a place cleared of all its occupants. It was, after all, privately owned and not a permanent military establishment, nor was it ever intended to be.

The account below appeared in the Saturday, 14 December 1918 edition of the *Denbighshire Free Press*:

GERMAN EXODUS FROM DYFFRYN ALED

During Sunday morning, excitement was occasioned by the passing through town to the railway station of a large number of army horse lorries in charge of soldiers from Dyffryn Aled laden with personal belongings of all kinds of the German prisoners at Dyffryn Aled Camp. On Tuesday morning, a batch of 133 German prisoners of war left the above internment camp for Oswestry, and it is understood that the camp will be closed at the end of this month. Their departure was witnessed with considerable satisfaction in this district, and the people generally hope that the day is not far distant when the other German prisoners of war, working about this district, will be cleared out and never be allowed to return.

Once all German prisoners of war and their guards had left, the Dyffryn Aled mansion was in a poor state of repair. Over four years of use as an internment camp had left it virtually uninhabitable, thereby spelling the beginning of the end for this formerly fine country mansion. POWs most certainly do not treat their prisons kindly.

First to be sold off from Dyffryn Aled were the hutments and building materials belonging to the military authorities, the details of which appeared in a number of local newspapers, including the Saturday, 28 June 1919 edition of the *Denbighshire Free Press*:

DYFFRYN ALED CAMP
SALE OF HUTMENTS, BUILDING MATERIALS ETC.

Messrs Clough & Co conducted a very important sale at Dyffryn Aled, Llansannan on Thursday by order of the Disposal Board of the War Office. The sale attracted a very large crowd and the bidding from the commencement was exceedingly keen. Every one of the lots were sold.

The first lot offered was a wooden barrack hut in six sections, with warming stove, piping and other utensils. This was sold for £100. A similar erection, but of a non-sectional character was knocked down for £115 and Captain Goronwy Griffith, Denbigh, secured two others for £115 each. Another building which had served as officers' quarters and comprising of a block of five separate dwelling apartments went for £300, and Mr Seele for Messrs Smart & Jones, Forest, Llansannan, bought the building known as 'The Hospital' for £360.

Other lots sold at high prices and about 60 miles of barbed wire were acquired by local farmers.

With the Dyffryn Aled mansion now in a poor condition internally, it was not in a fit state to rent out. The owner therefore decided to sell off the mansion and extensive grounds 'lock, stock and barrel'. The preliminary notice of the sale appeared in the *North Wales Chronicle* newspaper of Friday, 1 August 1919:

PRELIMINARY NOTICE
COUNTY OF DENBIGH
About eight miles from Denbigh and Abergele
IMPORTANT SALE of the GRAND FREEHOLD
RESIDENTIAL SPORTING and AGRICULTURAL
ESTATE
of
'DYFFRYN ALED'
having an area of
4,400 ACRES
or thereabouts.

MESSRS WM. DEW & SON and R. ARTHUR JONES will shortly offer the above Estate for Sale.
For further Particulars apply: R. M. Thomas Esq. Twining Ruabon; Harold Edwards Esq, Agent Gwrych Castle, Castle Estate Office, Abergele: or to the Auctioneers at their offices, Bangor and Conway.

My wife's uncle, Robert Douglas Owen, formerly of Gilfach, Llansannan, informs me that a large wooden hut from

Dyffryn Aled found its way, in about 1920, to become Llansannan Village Hall. He remembers this bygone building, which was located near to the river, as being referred to as the 'YM' or 'YMCA'. It is therefore more than feasible to believe that it was the YMCA Hut from Dyffryn Aled, which had been there for the comfort of the soldiers on guard.

In the translated memoirs of Grand Admiral Alfred Peter Friedrich von Tirpitz, we are given an insight as to how relations between the British and German navies reached 'hate point' by the end of the First World War:

> ... *Admiral Beatty provides a painful example of this development; on August 28th, 1914, he signalled to the officers and men rescued from the sunken Mainz: 'I am proud to welcome such brave men on board my Squadron.' In November 1918 on the other hand, he issued orders to his own crews before their meetings with the German crews who were to deliver up their ships: 'Never forget that the enemy is a despicable beast.'*

The German High Seas Fleet was, under the terms of the Armistice, 'interned' at Scapa Flow, Orkney Islands, Scotland, while negotiations as to their eventual fate were taking place. Germany's Admiral Ludwig von Reuter, fearing that the seventy-four ships would be seized as 'spoils of war' and divided between the victors, gave orders for all of them to be scuttled. This was carried out on 21 June 1919, but the British ships 'guarding' them managed to save twenty-two by beaching them. Over the following years, some of the scuttled German ships were salvaged and towed away for scrap, while those left are popular with underwater divers.

The defeated German Admiral Reinhard Scheer haughtily declared, after the events of 21 June 1919:

I rejoice, the stain of surrender has been wiped from the escutcheons of the German Fleet. The sinking of the ships has proved that the spirit of the fleet is not dead. The last act is true to the best traditions of the German Navy.

In reality, the performance of the Imperial Germany Navy in the First World War, apart from the great success of the U-Boats, had been a disaster, and the likes of Admiral Scheer knew it!

Chapter Twelve

Other Camps

Accounts from other camps in North Wales

The following is from the *Flintshire Observer* of Thursday, 13 August 1914:

> *A disused engineering works on the banks of the Dee between Sandycroft and Queensferry have been taken over by the Military Authorities as a place of detention for German prisoners of war. Already a large number are detained there and they are guarded by the Chester Company of the 5th Battalion, Cheshire Regiment.*

The *Denbighshire Free Press* of Saturday, 15 August 1914 reported the following in relation to the Queensferry, North East Wales, German POW and civilian internment camp:

> *GERMAN PRISONERS*

> *Colonel T. A. Wynne-Edwards has been assigned the Command of the troops engaged in the custody of German prisoners apprehended in this country. Over 200 have been brought down under guard to this district. The large works at Flintshire being formed into a concentration camp being used for their safekeeping. Col Wynne-Edwards is there in Command commencing on Monday.*

The *Herald of Wales* of Saturday, 15 August 1914 informed readers that many German prisoners from their locality (the areas of Swansea and the South Wales Valleys) were bound for an internment camp in North East Wales – the newly prepared Queensferry internment camp:

GERMAN SEAMEN TAKEN AWAY UNDER ESCORT

Escorted by an armed guard, with fixed bayonets, the German prisoners of war who were incarcerated in the Rutland Street Schools, left Swansea for the concentration camp at Queensferry, near Chester.

A large crowd gathered on the route to the G. W. Railway Station, but there was no hostile demonstration.

There were 85 prisoners in all, comprised of officers (sixteen) and men from ships in Swansea, Port Talbot and Briton Ferry Docks and they were accompanied by Mr C. Ludlow Livingstone, U.S.A., Consul at Swansea, who is watching the interests of German subjects in the town and district.

In conversation with several of the prisoners of war, we were informed that they had nothing but praise for the way in which they were treated while at the schools. The officers were kept apart from the men and had their food served separately. The rations were such as would be served to officers and men of the British Army, and were supplied under the direction of Major Llewellyn Thomas, Quartermaster to the 6th Welsh. For instance, while for dinner the officers would have beef-steak, potatoes, beans or peas, the men would have corned beef, potatoes and bread. 'If we are treated as well where we are going as we have been here, we shall be well off – except that we are prisoners', said one of the men.

Rations were also supplied for the prisoners on the journey. It may be added that none of the prisoners were residents of Swansea.

The *North Wales Chronicle* of Friday, 21 August 1914 had this on the Queensferry Camp:

> *It is understood that there are now about 1,000 German prisoners at the disused engineering works of Messrs Willans and Robinson at Queensferry on the banks of the Dee. The works are surrounded by a fence and a force of Cheshire Territorials are guarding the place. The Germans, many of whom are in possession of large sums of money, are well treated and fed. They pass their time in athletic games. A question has been asked, why not utilise their services in the fields? Let them help the farmers get the corn in.*

A German baron at Queensferry

The *Flintshire Observer* of Thursday, 24 September 1914, had this:

> *THE GERMAN COMPOUND AT QUEENSFERRY*
> *Titled Prisoners*
>
> *It is stated that the number of prisoners in the German compound at Queensferry is now over 2,000, the accommodation being taxed to the utmost. During the past three weeks, hundreds of reservists of the German Army have been admitted. Among those recently admitted is Baron von Trutzschler, who is well known in the hunting fields of Cheshire and Shropshire. He came to this country about fifteen years ago, settling down eventually at a hunting box at Norton-in-Hales, on the Cheshire and Shropshire borders, which he occupied on a lease. He was an extensive buyer of blood horses and hunters, and says the 'Manchester Guardian', it was an open secret that he bought them on commission for shipment to Germany. Some hundreds of horses must have passed through the Baron's hands during*

the last ten years. Of late years, he kept a German secretary at his hunting box at Norton-in-Hales. The secretary was a lieutenant in the German Army. When the war broke out the Baron's stables were visited by Lieutenant Armitage of the R.H.A. and a police officer. The Baron had then left. There were however sixteen hunters in his stables and these were commandeered for the British Army. The Baron's motor car was also requisitioned. There are also in the prison, it is stated, several others who bear German titles.

Baron Robert Franz Oswald Adolph von Trutzschler was born in Germany in 1877, and in 1906 he married British-born Katherine Murphy in the Nantwich Registration District. He would die at the Royal Infirmary, Chester, on 14 February 1940, aged sixty-two, leaving his estate to his widow, Baroness Katherine von Trutzschler.

The same edition of the *Flintshire Observer* as above also had the following article, which relates to the Queensferry Camp:

GERMANS LEAVE FOR ISLE OF MAN
From Queensferry and other Concentration Camps

About two hundred German prisoners gathered from Queensferry and other Concentration Camps in England and Scotland left Liverpool on Monday night for the Isle of Man, where it is understood they will be detained until the close of the war.

They seemed in excellent spirits and laughed and joked with the crowd of people who had gathered on the stage to witness their departure. Accompanied by a strong guard, the prisoners arrived at Riverside Station about ten o'clock and were escorted in small detachments down the bridge to the Isle of Man Steam Packet Company's Steamer, Tynwald.

The first indication of their arrival was the appearance on the landing stage of soldiers wheeling heavy trucks laden with baggage (says the Liverpool Daily Post). This was piled in a heap alongside the steamer and then the soldiers – porters, attacked the mountain of bags and boxes and stowed it away on the steamer in an amazingly short space of time. Porters 'by profession' could have learned a few tips from these soldiers.

Then came the order to 'fix bayonets'. Some of the soldiers mounted guard along the stage and round the gangway, while others returned to the station to escort the prisoners to the ship. In parties of seven or eight, preceded and followed by soldiers, the Germans filed down to the boat. Many of them were grotesquely clad; they were smoking almost to a man. They seemed quite subdued as they passed the grim-looking line of bayonets, but once on board the Tynwald they became quite merry. They lined the bulwarks and chatted to people on the stage. Most of them could speak English and they all seemed to know about the Isle of Man.

'We're just running over for a holiday', said a smiling-faced young fellow, who didn't seem to mind being a prisoner at all. Another was less friendly. 'England', he said, 'England is finished.'

'What's the matter with your Crown Prince?' retorted someone on the stage. 'Where's your navy?'

Another spectator called on the prisoners to do the 'goose-step', but one of them gravely declined.

'I do not know how to do it. I cannot dance', he said.

A few minutes later the rope was cast off; the crowds cheered as the last of the soldiers ran on board; and the Tynwald steamed down the river carrying to Manx-land the strangest company of visitors that has ever sailed for her shore. As the steamer disappeared in the darkness one could hear the voices of the German prisoners raised in discordant, but vigorous song.

The above recounts the start of the exodus from the British mainland for Germans (and certain other nationalities, such as Austrians) to the two newly formed internment camps on the Isle of Man, where many of the men would spend the next four or so years trying to forge out a new, semi-permanent lifestyle for themselves. For them it meant being separated from their wives, children and other loved ones.

The account below is from the *Haverfordwest and Milford Haven Telegraph* of Wednesday, 25 November 1914, and it demonstrates just how volatile things could get inside the civilian internment camps on the Isle of Man. Perhaps some killed or injured in this Douglas Camp 'revolt', as the press called it, had only recently arrived from the Queensferry Camp, North East Wales:

ALIEN CAMP RIOT
PRISONERS SHOT BY SENTRIES

Five alien enemy prisoners were killed and twelve injured as a result of a revolt last week in the detention camp at Douglas, Isle of Man, where there are about 4,000 interned men. Following complaints about the quality and quantity of food, the prisoners, it is said, threw plates, knives, forks, and chairs about the dining-room, and finally made a determined dash for the kitchens. The guards endeavoured to restore order by firing in the air and threatening the men with bayonets. These measures having failed, they were obliged to adopt sterner methods to subdue the rioters.

The camp was guarded by men drawn from The National Reserve and the Manx Territorials.

The local authorities, it should be added, deny that there were any grounds for the prisoners' complaints.

The Wednesday, 2 December 1914 edition of the same newspaper had this:

DOUGLAS CAMP RIOT

An exhaustive enquiry was conducted at Douglas on Friday, into the recent camp riot at the German Concentration Camp. The jury found that the deaths of the five prisoners was due to protective measures, which the riot compelled the military authorities to take. The Coroner expressed his complete agreement with the verdict.

The internment camp referred to in the above was located at the military authorities' requisitioned Cunningham's Holiday Camp. It was opened to house internees on 22 September 1914. This the smaller of the two such camps on the Isle of Man was allegedly where 'those with money' went.

The *Manchester Courier and Lancashire General Advertiser* of Thursday, 26 November 1914 gave an insight into everyday life for the 'various types' of internees at the Queensferry Detention Barracks, and some details regarding this large temporary camp itself:

In the concentration camp for prisoners of war at Queensferry, some ten miles from Chester, men and youths to the number of 2,200, are interned at a large disused factory. The factory covers so extensive an area, that it is found convenient to have two large compounds enclosed by barbed-wire fencing.

The prisoners entrusted to the care of the commandant and his staff include soldiers, but the great majority are officers and men of the German mercantile marine; clerks; members of hotel staffs; and professional and businessmen generally.

The correspondence passing through the camp post office, even with the limitation of two letters per man, totals weekly up to 2,500. This means that fully 1,750 have to be censored locally. A tour of the 'blocks' by a Press Association representative served to reveal something of the prevailing tone and temper of the camp. One section had indulged in a fancy-dress procession, a highly diverting exhibition of the grotesque in costume; another section was applying itself to open-air games with quite juvenile ardour. Under cover, separate bunks or berths, especially in the marine officers' quarters, boast such titles as 'Stadt Hamburg', 'Villa Germania', 'Villa Emden', and the 'Moulin Rouge'. Suspended from a crossbeam is a model of Captain von Muller's famous cruiser 'Emden'.

A number of the interned devote themselves most diligently to constructing models, mostly of steam or sailing ships, and derive some profit from their work by offering their handiwork to the highest bidders. Some less mechanical, turn to undertake outside labour such as levelling, laying ashes, using the tar brush, and so forth. An attempt has been made to put a stop to this particular branch of activity. The objectors are the Trade Unions, and they protest on the ground that the labourers are not paid the trade union rate.

During a somewhat prolonged stay within the compound, a number of the men were questioned by the writer. But nothing in the nature of a serious complaint was voiced. The one instance in which a word of criticism was uttered was that of a merchant skipper, and what he said had reference to the alleged treatment of him at Cardiff before he was taken off to Queensferry. His complaint is that the police authorities are too alert – that they bottled him up without affording him the chance of giving them the slip.

'But Captain', I ventured to suggest, 'you would probably

agree with me, that what you don't know about the Bristol Channel port, is not worth knowing.'

'You may be right there', he answered with a hearty laugh.

'Ah then', I remarked, *'the authorities thought you were a fitting subject for attention.'*

An opportunity was given for witnessing drill. The squads were truly international – Prussian infantrymen, alien Turks, and alien Jews, wheeled and deployed side by side. Some of these men are by no means dependent upon the daily ration, good as it admittedly is. Five of them on admission totalled up £300 in cash. It is prisoners so situated who can take full advantage of the canteen, where special tariff lists are posted. I was told of the case of a British prisoner interned in Germany, who has made it known, that he and his fellows can get neither meat or butter, nor milk. The fact that at Queensferry, as well as at all the concentration camps, there is a proposal to add peas, beans, and lentils or rice to the existing ration, makes the contrast all the worse.

Over 700 pairs of good strong boots have been recently given out of the stores. Of these, 240 pairs were distributed at the end of last week, and the Quartermaster has started the issue of another 177 pairs. The Commandant puts no restriction on the quantity of presents and 'games' sent in. One of the interned is a German pastor. He was given a chance of freedom, but his reply was, 'I prefer to remain. I can do much better work here than outside', and so he preaches and distributes literature.

Death at the Queensferry Camp
The *Flintshire Observer* of Thursday, 26 November 1914 had this:

QUEENSFERRY
GERMAN PRISONER'S DEATH

Mr E. Brassey, City Coroner, held an inquest at the Infirmary, on Thursday, concerning the death of Walter Sick, a German, of 10, Oxford Grove, Chorlton-on-Medlock. He was 23 years of age and had been a hotel chef. It appeared that the deceased had been removed from Manchester on the 22nd October to the compound at Queensferry, and on the 25th he was taken ill. Two days later he was removed to Chester Infirmary, where he underwent an operation for appendicitis and died on Wednesday. The Coroner said it was a very plain case, but he held the Inquest in compliance with a Home Office circular. Dr Herbert, the Government Medical Officer at Queensferry, diagnosed the case as one of acute appendicitis, and on his arrival at Chester the deceased was seen by Dr Henry Dobie and Dr Leahy, House Surgeon, who confirmed the nature of the complaint. The man himself requested the operation and told the House Surgeon that he had had the complaint before. Deceased spoke English perfectly. Evidence of identification was given by the widow, Eva Sick, who is an English woman and who said she was married on the 25th August 1913. In reply to the Coroner, she said he had not been in the German Army. He left Germany when he was 13 years of age. He was not naturalised as he had not been in England long enough, having resided here only four years. After leaving Germany he went to Switzerland, where he resided for a time and afterwards to France. Deceased's father was Karl Sick, a Master Confectioner. She did not know that her husband had had an attack before of appendicitis. She saw him before the operation and he seemed quite confident he would pull through. She was getting relief at the rate of 10 s. per week from the American

Consul. In reply to the Coroner, she said that she did not suppose that she would get relief now that her husband was dead. Mr Brassey advised the woman to apply to the English Poor Law Authorities. Dr Leahy, House Surgeon, said the man was seen by himself and Dr Henry Dobie and appeared to understand that his life depended upon the operation, and said he had a previous attack in the Canary Islands. Deceased himself wanted the operation. Dr Dobie operated. They found that the appendix was 'inflamed, but there was nothing inside'. There was a certain amount of scar which indicated a previous attack. Death took place as a result of peritonitis following appendicitis. The Jury returned a verdict of 'death from natural causes'.

In 1891, Walter Sick had been born in Germany to Karle Sick, a confectioner. He married Eva Weatherill on 25 August 1913 at St Michael's Parish Church, Hulme, Manchester. At the time of their marriage, the couple resided at 16 Clare Street, Denton, Manchester.

By the middle of September 1914, the Queensferry Camp now 'accommodated' over 2,000 internees, with more arriving daily. As such, those who had been at the camp for a number of weeks were being moved to more permanent camps. The Royal Welch Fusiliers continued to provide the majority of the guards.

The *Denbighshire Free Press* of Saturday, 5 December 1914 reported that Mr C. C. Mott, who was 'so well known in the Vale of Clwyd', had been appointed, with the rank of captain, as second-in-command at the Queensferry Detention Barracks.

The closure of Queensferry Detention Barracks

The *Denbighshire Free Press* of Saturday, 15 May 1915 printed the following in relation to the Queensferry Camp:

Farewell Orders by Lieutenant-Colonel A. Reed, DSO., VD., Commandant, Queensferry, 12th May 1915

The camp is now breaking up and though some detachments will be left until next week, one, the 7th Cheshire's, will leave here tomorrow.

Before we all go I should like to express my appreciation of what has been done by the officers, non-commissioned officers, and by men of the troops in carrying out the work of guarding the prisoners.

I wish to say how much I recognise the loyal obedience to my orders and the careful manner the various duties have been carried out under all conditions.

You are not young men but men of mature age, whose habits and thoughts are deep rooted and therefore your return to duty, with its irksomeness, is all the more creditable; and I fully realise how hard and monotonous the work here has been, and wish to congratulate you, and thank you for supporting me and the officers in all that has been asked of you.

I part with you all with great reluctance and feel it very much that we all have to disperse, but wherever you are, and whatever you are doing, I trust that all will be well with you, and that your training here will be good fruit in your new posts.

A new internment camp

News of a new internment camp for 'alien subjects' in North Wales was reported on in the *Flintshire Observer* of Thursday, 8 July 1915:

Internment Camp near Mold
Building formerly used as a Jesuit College and Convent

The War Office have completed arrangements whereby they will be enabled to enter into the occupation of the Convent near Mold, as an internment camp for alien enemies.

The new camp's buildings were built in 1874, erected by the Flintshire Quarter Sessions to take the place of the obsolete county gaol at Flint. The Mold gaol had been used for the reception and detention of prisoners, but some years ago it was closed by order of the Home Office. Next it was used as a Jesuit College and later, following the burning of the Roman Catholic reformatory ship, 'the Clarence' in the Mersey, it was temporarily used as a reformatory school. Lastly, and up to a few years ago, the property served the purpose of a convent for a French Roman Catholic society.

Captured near Wrexham

The *Llangollen Advertiser* of Friday, 21 April 1916 had this account:

German Prisoners Captured Near Wrexham

Considerable excitement was caused at Wrexham, on Saturday night, when it became known that the four German prisoners, who had escaped on Thursday from the Frongoch Camp, Bala, had been seen in the neighbourhood of Bwlchgwyn. The police redoubled the efforts they had been making throughout the day, and a party of special constables were employed to search several parts of the district. Mr Hugh Jones of Llandegla, who had read in the daily papers a description of the missing Germans, seeing four men on the moors, he at once sent word to PC Howell Edwards of Bwlchgwyn, who eventually discovered them lying amongst the heather between Llandegla and Rhydtalog. Lance-Corporal Lee and Private Davies of the 2nd R.W.F., had taken part in the search over the moors which lasted several hours.

When spoken to by Mr Hugh Jones, the Germans did not reply, but returned to the moor. Later, they were surrounded and caught. They gave Welsh surnames, but on the officer challenging them one said, 'It's all right. We have made a mistake walking in the day time.' The men were afterwards taken to Wrexham by DCC Tippett and PC Edwards, and they remained in the County Buildings until Monday morning, when they were marched to the GWR station under military escort and taken back to Bala. The men had food and money in their possession, and were provided with a compass and an accurate map of North Wales and the border country. They stated that they were making for Liverpool.

These four German POW escapers had all been taken prisoner at Neuve Chapelle, France, in March of 1915.

Put to work
This article appeared in the Friday, 9 November 1917 edition of the *North Wales Chronicle*:

PENMAENMAWR AND GERMAN PRISONERS
QUARRYMEN'S PROTEST

Preparations are being made at Penmaenmawr for the housing there of a number of German prisoners of war who are to be employed in the granite quarries.

At the meeting of the Penmaenmawr Council on Tuesday night, Mr R. D. Owen in the chair, Mr Griffith Roberts, a Labour member, moved that the Council protest strongly the employment of German labour in the quarries. The motion was seconded by Mr T. Roberts.

Speaking in opposition to the resolution, Mr P. H. McClement said the Government seemed to think that it would be to their advantage to employ 144 Germans there. All the available labour was already engaged in the quarries, but the quantity of material the Government required was not being produced, with the result that the Government were going to the expense of fencing with barbed wire the place in which the prisoners would be billeted. He understood that the stone from Penmaenmawr was to be used near Liverpool. Certainly, the Government would not wish to send prisoners to Penmaenmawr if it were not for some good reason. He suggested that it was outside the jurisdiction of the Council to pass the resolution which had been proposed. It was a 'dog in the manger' policy to protest against these men being brought to the quarry to assist the Government in getting the material necessary to carry on the war. He understood that a deputation from the Quarrymen's Union had been down to consider the matter, but they had not sent any direct communication to the Council.

Mr Griffith Roberts said there had been a general meeting in the quarry, at which the Secretary of the Union had been called in. Every hand was up against these Germans coming there, and if they came there would be trouble.

Mr J. H. Higson, who is one of the Directors of the Quarry Company explained that although the quarry was not 'controlled' by the Government, the output had to be disposed of according to Government directions. The company had tried to get some of their own men back from the army, but the Government would not consent to that and said that they would supply German prisoners. If they came, the prisoners would be an advantage to the whole neighbourhood; they would enable the quarries to be kept working better and better wages would be earned by the present staff.

The resolution was defeated by a majority of one.

The Friday, 23 November 1917 edition of the *North Wales Chronicle* further reported upon the matter:

PENMAENMAWR
QUARRYMEN AND THE EMPLOYMENT OF ENEMY
PRISONERS

A well-attended meeting of local Quarrymen was held on Saturday in Ebenezer Chapel to consider the attitude of the local Unionists towards the proposed employment of German Prisoners in the local quarries.

Escape!

The *North Wales Chronicle* newspaper of Friday, 31 May 1918 had this:

ESCAPED GERMAN PRISONERS RECAPTURED IN ANGLESEY

Three German prisoners who escaped from the internment camp at Llangaffo, Anglesey, were recaptured yesterday in the neighbourhood of Plas Coch.

The *Abergavenny Chronicle* of Friday, 22 February 1918 reported upon the jailing of three women from North East England for helping two German civilian escapees from a North Wales internment camp:

HARBOURED GERMAN PRISONERS

Three women were sentenced to imprisonment by West Hartlepool Magistrates for harbouring two German civilian prisoners who had escaped from a camp in Flintshire. One prisoner had obtained a seaman's discharge book. It was stated that both men could speak English well.

The *Llangollen Advertiser* of Friday, 27 September 1918 reported another escape by German POWs, this time from a working party at Corwen:

MERIONETHSHIRE

Three prisoners of war are reported to have escaped from a working party at Corwen on Monday. They are Wilhelm Newhaus, a German, aged 24, medium build, complexion fair and pale, clean shaven, wearing trousers with red patch. Alfred Zimbel, German, aged 21, medium build, complexion fair, light-red hair, freckles, clean shaven, speaks a little English, wearing trousers with red patches. Also, Eugene Kiles, German, aged 24, medium build, mark under eye, small moustache, complexion dark, wearing trousers with red patches, and speaks a little English.

A camp near Ruthin.

The *Denbighshire Free Press* newspaper of Sunday, 28 July 1918 contained this:

BATHAFARN HALL GERMAN POW CAMP
GERMAN PRISONERS OF WAR

A large number of people assembled at the Railway Station, Ruthin, on Saturday afternoon to witness the arrival of some German prisoners of war, who were being taken to the Internment Camp at Bathafarn.

About 30 prisoners arrived and were escorted by a military guard to their quarters. A few of them were of very youthful appearance.

It is understood that they will be engaged by farmers in the district for work in the harvest.

Bathafarn Hall was a fine, large mansion in quite stunning countryside at Llanbedr Dyffryn Clwyd, near Ruthin. The estate had been put on the market in 1899 as it was heavily mortgaged, but it failed to reach its reserve price. The military authorities took over (officially commandeered) and prepared Bathafarn Hall as an internment camp for German POWs from mid-1918. Some months after the Armistice, the military authorities returned Bathafarn Hall to its owners, and in October 1919, it was sold off with Llanbedr Hall.

Shot dead

In late October 1918, at the non-officer internment camp at Machynlleth, Wales, an incident occurred which resulted in the violent death of one of the German POWs. *The Cambrian News and Merionethshire Standard* of Friday, 1 November 1918 very prominently carried an account which included the details of the coroner's inquest:

GERMAN PRISONER SHOT
REFUSED TO HALT WHEN CHALLENGED BY
SENTRY

A sensation was caused at Machynlleth on Monday when it became known that one of the German prisoners at the internment camp had been shot the previous evening.

The German, Walter Willie Herbert Gribenow, was, it is said, found outside the boundary and disregarding the challenge of a sentry, which was given three times, was shot, and died instantaneously.

An inquest was held on Tuesday by Dr David Edwards,

Coroner. The Jury were Messrs A. Gribble (Foreman), W. P. Evans, David Owen, John Thomas, W. M. Jones, Alfred Jones, J. J. Owen and Owen Davies.

Capt. John Burgess read the standing order in relation to prisoners of war, which stated that any prisoner attempting to escape, or out of boundary would after being challenged once, be fired on if he disregarded the challenge. E. Stehr, who described himself as a Prussian, and gave his evidence in good English, said he acted as interpreter. The deceased was 24 and a private, a native of Hanover. No regulations were posted up in the camp, but some were posted up in German at the Frongoch Camp from where the prisoners came in August. Deceased knew of these regulations because the prisoners were told before leaving Frongoch that the same regulations would be in force.

A Juryman: 'Would the deceased understand the challenge?'

Witness: 'Yes. The word "halt" is similar to the German word, and the pronunciation is alike.'

The Foreman: 'Could the deceased understand English?'

Witness: 'Yes, very well.'

After giving his evidence witness turned to leave the room, but the Coroner told him he could stay if he desired, and he stayed till the end.

Dr W. R. Williams, Medical Officer, said he was summoned on Sunday evening and found the deceased lying huddled up on his left side on the ground about forty yards from the main road. Blood was oozing from his mouth, and when witness examined him he found life extinct. Death must have been instantaneous.

A Juryman: 'Anyone happening to pass along the road at the time might have been hit by the bullet?'

Witness: Yes.

[A Juryman:] 'In your opinion was the deceased coming

towards or going from the camp?'
  [Witness:] 'Coming towards it.'
  The Coroner: 'How do you form that opinion?'
  Witness: 'From the position of the body.'

In reply to further questions Dr Williams said the night was very dark moonless and starless.

Private William Davies who wore two wound stripes said he was on guard when he heard a whistle from the front end of the camp and another from the direction of the road. He went towards the road and found Gribenow about 80 yards from the boundary post. He challenged him and receiving no reply fired. When he went to him, Gribenow groaned twice.

The Coroner: 'What distance were you from him when you fired?

Witness: About 15 yards.'

[The Coroner:] 'Did you recognise him?'

[Witness:] 'Yes, by his clothes.'

[The Coroner:] 'Did you miss the prisoner last night?'

[Witness:] 'No sir.'

Witness added that it was a starlit night, and that he could see forty yards. When Dr Williams came to the camp it was raining and very dark.

The Foreman: 'Are the prisoners allowed to go beyond the boundary?'

Witness: 'No sir.'

Witness in reply to further questions said Gribenow was going in the direction of the hills. He challenged him three times, but he did not stop.

Mr Owen, Postmaster: 'Are the Guards not to be inside the boundary when they fire?'

The Coroner: 'You cannot discuss that.'

Mr Owen (to Davies): 'You knew whom you were shooting?'

Witness: 'Yes.'

Sergeant Wilfred Moore, in charge of the guards, said that he had told the guards that if one of the prisoners attempted to escape he was to be challenged, and if he disregarded the challenge the guard was to fire.

PC Humphreys said the deceased was found about 81 yards outside the boundary and about 30 yards from the road.

Coroner said it was evident the deceased knew the regulations, yet he went outside the camp and after being challenged three times by the sentry failed to respond. According to the evidence the man died from injuries received from a bullet wound after being shot down by a sentry whilst attempting to escape, and after having been duly challenged.

Some of the jurymen demurred at the word 'escape', and the Coroner said that according to the evidence the man was going in the direction of the hills and the assumption was that he was trying to escape.

Mr Owen: 'The word "escape" we do not like.'

The Coroner: 'I am afraid you have preconceived ideas. You can form your own opinion according to the evidence. I have formed mine.'

In the end, the Jury returned a verdict on the lines indicated by the Coroner, and added a rider that the notice of the Military Authorities be drawn to the dangers for pedestrians owing to the close proximity of the camp to the main road.

'Nobody knows', said the Foreman, 'what might have happened on this dark night had anyone been passing when the sentry shot. The bullet might have found another billet.'

One of the jurymen thought the camp should be enclosed, but Capt. Burgess stated that definite orders had been received from the military authorities that no camps were to be enclosed.

The Coroner: 'And the prisoners are very thankful that they are not enclosed.'

The Juryman: 'But it is dangerous. Only the other day a boy went through the camp and he might have been shot.'

The Coroner: 'I am afraid you are hypersensitive here.'

This 'shooting and killing' incident was not an isolated one. At the post-Armistice camp at Park Hall, near Oswestry, just over the border from Wales, a German POW named Willy Oster was shot and killed on 12 July 1919, by a guard at the camp. It was alleged that during some 'disturbances' in the camp Willy Oster had thrown a brick at a guard, and that this guard on sentry duty had shot him dead with one shot from his rifle. This resulted in further disturbances at the camp, with the German POWs, led by their officers, refusing to attend roll calls. As a result, to help restore order, the Royal Defence Corps were drafted in.

At the subsequent coroner's inquest, it was stated on the British side that a guard on sentry duty had been pelted with stones thrown by a number of German POWs, and that the guard, in order to summon assistance, had fired into the air and inadvertently hit, with fatal results, Willy Oster, aged but twenty, who happened to be standing on a nearby roof! Whatever the true facts of the matter were, Willy Oster was dead, and the inquest returned a verdict of 'death by misadventure'.

In 1967, all German servicemen and civilian internees who had been buried in the various graveyards around Britain during both world wars were removed to the newly created German Military Cemetery at Cannock Chase, Staffordshire. Musketier Willy Oster was re-buried at this cemetery in Plot 12, Row 5, Grave 149.

Because Germany had 'lost the war', German POWs in Britain post-Armistice continued to be treated as POWs into late 1919. It was only then that most of them were finally repatriated back to the Fatherland. The *North Wales Chronicle*, in their edition of 21 November 1919, reported on the closure of the Fron Goch Camp near Bala. It reported that the last batch of German POWs, numbering 2,280, were despatched earlier that week. This camp had been used back in 1914 for German POWs, then for a time in 1916 for Irish Republican prisoners, and then again for German POWs.

Chapter Thirteen

Husbands and Wives

How 'alien men' and their British-born wives fared

The 'British Nationality and Status of Aliens Act' was brought into existence by the British government on 7 August 1914, just a few days after the First World War began. This act superseded the 'Aliens Act' of 1905, and introduced far more restrictive provisions. It remained in force until it was repealed post-First World War by the enacting of the 'Aliens Restriction (Amendment) Act' of 1919.

The intention of the 'British Nationality and Status of Aliens Act' was to provide stronger and more extensive powers to deal with so-called 'enemy aliens'. Foreign-born persons who were resident in Britain were required to register themselves, and to possess a valid 'alien registration card', which was to be available for inspection by the authorities at any time. It also continued the practice of discriminating against British-born women who were married to foreign-born men (generally German, Austrian or Hungarian), while favouring foreign-born women who were married to British-born men. This can be evidenced by reading the Act itself:

PART III
GENERAL

10. National Status of Married Women
Subject to the provisions of this Section, the wife of a British Subject shall be deemed to be a British Subject, and the wife of an alien shall be deemed to be an alien.

From the outset of the war, the British government and the British press played a leading role in stirring up the people against Germany and the Central Powers. Such anti-German and 'anti-alien' propaganda greatly aided military recruitment in Britain, and ensured that the British public 'knuckled' down and continued to exude wartime fervour.

The British government even set-up a 'secret' propaganda agency to create anti-German and Central Powers feeling, especially among the working class, whom they believed (generally correctly) would be very susceptible to such misinformation. It was called the British War Propaganda Bureau (WPB), and known covertly as 'Wellington House'. It was run by Charles Frederick Gurney Masterman (1873-1927), a radical-thinking Liberal politician who worked closely with David Lloyd George and Winston Churchill. Apparently, no anti-enemy story was beyond their remit. Masterman got on board at the WPB such high-profile and respected writers of the time as John Buchan, Arthur Conan Doyle and H.G. Wells, to assist in the bureau's efforts.

It was Masterman who commissioned the 1916 film *The Battle of the Somme*. First released on 10 August 1916, it was both documentary and propaganda. Filmed by two official war cinematographers, it is an amazing example of cinema for its time, and actually shows the trenches, marching British infantry, the treatment of wounded British and German soldiers, the shelling of German positions, and the German dead and their captured trenches. It is worth noting that a scene in the film where British soldiers 'go over the top' towards the enemy was staged safely behind the British lines! But nevertheless, it became a sensation, with an estimated twenty million British people watching it in cinemas across the length and breadth of the country. The film was also shown in eighteen other countries. It lasts for seventy-seven minutes and originally consisted of five reels of film. Though a propaganda film, today it is regarded as being of great historical significance.

A mere eight days after the declaration of war, the incident described below occurred. The article is taken from the *North Wales Chronicle* of Friday, 14 August 1914, and it shows just how quickly an individual was able to become an 'alien enemy', even if they were of means.

GERMAN MOTORIST HELD UP AT CRICCIETH

A German motorist came to Criccieth on Wednesday and P.C. Hugh Thomas seized his car. Later the German saw the Chief Constable and Supt Owen and he produced his registration certificate and was allowed to use his motor car within the five-mile radius.

In the same edition of the newspaper, there was also this:

GERMAN TENT ON THE GREAT ORME
SEIZURE OF ARMS BY THE LLANDUDNO POLICE

A military rifle and a quantity of ammunition have been seized from a German by the Llandudno Police. Shortly after ten o'clock on Monday night, Sergeant Richards and a police constable visited Pyllau Farm on the Great Orme, in search of a German named Hammond, who they understood was staying at the farm. They found Hammond, who appeared to be a man about 45 years of age and was employed as a hairdresser in the town. He did not deny his nationality, but stated that he had registered himself at the Conwy police station, which was afterwards found to be correct.

The German had erected a tent at the rear of the house in

which a military rifle and a box of ammunition was discovered and seized by the police. The man gave up his ammunition without any hesitation when requested to do so by the police. He still follows his employment as a hairdresser.

This, we believe, is the first seizure of arms in Caernarfonshire.

The Bettin family

The Bettin family ran the popular Ferry Hotel in Talycafn, the Conway Valley, North Wales. The public first heard of their 'difficulties' on 10 August 1914, when the Conway Police visited, though one might fairly say 'raided', their establishment. Once inside, the authorities took possession of rifles and ammunition belonging to the German-born hotelier Otto Carl Paul Bettin, who subsequently contacted the local press himself, and informed them of the seizure of his motor vehicle. A few days later, he would be arrested and interned by the authorities, though this was certainly not the end of matters.

The Ferry Hotel, Tal y Cafn, Conwy Valley

On Friday, 23 October 1914, the *North Wales Chronicle* reported on the question of the Ferry Hotel's license being brought up at the Llandudno Magistrates Court:

GERMAN HOTEL KEEPER AND HIS LICENCE TALYCAFN HOTEL DIFFICULTY

At the Llandudno Petty Sessions on Monday, before Dr Dalton (Chairman) and other magistrates.

Mr E. W. Johnson mentioned the case of Mrs Bettin, which had been adjourned from the last sessions and which was an application for the transfer of the licence of the Ferry Hotel, Talycafn, from her husband, Otto Bettin, to her name. Mr Bettin, a German, was now interned. Mr Johnson had told his client that he would not apply for a transfer to her and that he had suggested that her best plan would be to find someone British to have the licence transferred to. The hotel belonged to General Gough and Mr Bettin had it under a lease. Mr Bettin was negotiating for the sale of the lease and in the meantime a receiver was to be appointed in the person of Mr J. H. Jones, Accountant, Llandudno. He applied to the court to transfer the licence to Mr J. H. Jones as the receiver, and that Mrs Bettin and her mother who now occupied the hotel, should leave the premises.

The Chairman said the magistrates did not feel that they were called upon to protect the interests of an alien enemy. The case would therefore be adjourned for another two weeks and if no suitable tenant was found by then the licence would elapse. The Bench also thought it was very unsatisfactory that the alien enemy's wife should have been suggested as a licensee.

Mr E. W. Johnson said he hoped that Bench understood that he was not applying for the transfer to Mrs Bettin.

Mr Henry Jones, Llanrwst, said he appeared on behalf of

the owner of the property to say that the wishes of the magistrates would be carried out in every respect as far as the owner was concerned.

The *Flintshire Observer* of Thursday, 5 November 1914 gave details of Otto Bettin's whereabouts and the fate of the Ferry Hotel, Talycafn, which the Bettin's had been running successfully for a number of years:

ALIEN'S HOTEL LICENCE TRANSFERRED

The licence of the Ferry Hotel, Talycafn, was transferred by the Conway Magistrates on Monday, from Otto Bettin, a German subject at present interned as a prisoner of war at Queensferry, to Theodore Martin, Liscard, Cheshire, an ex-captain of the Union Castle line of steamships.

With her German husband interned for the foreseeable future and almost certainly for the duration of the war, it was a harsh result and price being paid by Mrs Christina Gertrude Bettin, born and bred in Manchester, England. With their business now gone, it meant that she and her elderly widowed mother, Emily Maria Holtkamp, who lived with them at the Ferry Hotel, were now homeless. All this caused misery and great uncertainty for her and her mother, all because she had married a German man.

Otto Carl Paul Bettin was born in 1873, in Hanover, Germany. In the June quarter of 1909, in the Manchester Registration District, he had married Christina Gertrude Holtkamp.

Christina Gertrude Holtkamp was born in Manchester on 9 June 1881, to John Henry Holtkamp, a Hanover, German-born cook and publican, and his Manchester-born wife, Emily Maria Holtkamp (nee Rigby).

The 1911 Census shows us that Otto Bettin was the hotel proprietor of the commodious twenty-roomed Ferry Hotel at Talycafn, North Wales. At the time it was taken, three servant staff were employed there, as well as his wife, and a boarder was in the premises. 'Talycafn' translates into English as 'place opposite the ferry-boat', as it was once an important stopping point for ferry traffic up and down the river. The Ferry Hotel, situated on the banks, was a popular destination for ferry passengers, with it having tea gardens which meandered down to the water's edge.

Other instances of anti-German sentiment

The following is from the *North Wales Chronicle* of Friday, 4 September 1914:

GERMAN ARRESTED AT PENRHYNDEUDRAETH

The arrest of a German named Henri Gustav Millar late on Monday caused quite a sensation at Penrhyndeudraeth.
The inhabitants of Upper Penrhyn, on seeing a foreign-looking man loitering near Penybwlch Station all day on Monday, informed the police, who about 11.00 p.m. effected an arrest. When taken into custody he admitted to being a German. On the following day, he was sentenced to one month's imprisonment for failing to register himself.

The *Barmouth and County Advertiser* of Thursday, 24 September 1914 had the following, which concerns foreign persons and their eligibility to vote:

GERMAN AND HIS WELSH WIFE

The extraordinary fact was disclosed at Penrhyndeudraeth Revision Court on Tuesday, that a German subject, on marrying a Welsh girl, had assumed the name of John Roberts and had been on the register for three years. He was objected to as an alien and his name was struck off the register. Another German subject's claim to a vote was also disallowed.

The *Flintshire Observer* of Thursday, 22 October 1914 had this on anti-German 'problems' in Flint, North Wales:

ANTI-GERMAN MOVE AT FLINT
Resident's Hostile Demonstration Against Aliens
TWENTY-FOUR HOURS NOTICE TO QUIT
Deputations to the Mayor and the Police
EXTRAORDINARY SCENES

Remarkable scenes took place at Flint on Monday night. A demonstration against the presence of men of German nationality residing in the town.

The demonstrations have from time to time been made since August last, but up to the present they were not regarded with much concern.

The contention among Flint people appears to be that some of the men to whom they object have behaved in a manner that did not tend to engender good feeling and lacked discretion.

It is alleged that some time ago a man in a public place trampled and spat upon the British flag. Such an act could not be tolerated by Flint men and he was compelled to pick up the flag and kiss it. Around that incident built up many stories.

On Saturday night, there was an inclination to take summary steps to rid the borough of aliens, but other counsels prevailed.

Between Saturday and Monday evening, a notice was

posted on a window in the town that efforts would be made to remove Germans in the town and that they would leave at seven o'clock for the compound at Queensferry.

By seven o'clock crowds of people assembled in the vicinity of the railway station, but there was no appearance of the removal of anyone to the compound. Later in the evening a deputation of residents waited on the Mayor at the Town Hall and intimated that they 'wanted to have the Germans removed'.

The Mayor advised them to consult him the following morning or to get into consultation with the Chief Constable. The deputation retired and the Chief Constable was consulted over the telephone. A meeting was held in the square and speeches were made and newspaper descriptions of the London and Edinburgh affairs were read to the crowd. Following upon that the crowd marched in procession to the houses of where Germans were known to reside. The occupants were not seen, but the message was left that they were given twenty-four hours to leave the town. The crowd had a threatening attitude. Inspector Williams and the men under him exercised admirable control and discretion in dealing with the incident until finally the crowd dispersed.

On Tuesday afternoon at the police station, a deputation of local residents with Councillor R. W. Barber as spokesman, held an interview with Superintendent R. Yarnell Davies, Mold, and Inspector J. Williams, Flint. Dr J. Humphrey Williams, Flint, was also present.

The deputation pointed out that the presence of Germans in the town was obnoxious to the townspeople and the feeling was becoming intensified from various causes.

Under the circumstances, it was considered advisable that the authorities should take steps to deal with such persons and by the means in their power remove from Flint the danger of any breach of the peace.

They explained what had occurred and how far the sentiment of the crowd had been repressed, but could not say how far they could keep control over people who were disposed to resent the presence of aliens in their midst.

Superintendent Davies explained to the deputation the position of the authorities with regard to the orders from the Home Office. The persons to whom exception was taken were duly registered aliens, and had so far complied with the requirements under the alien's restriction orders.

It was explained to the deputation that arrangements were being made, by which it was hoped the popular objection to the people would be overcome.

The works were not German works and Dr Andraea was an Englishman, who, he believed, had a brother serving in the Naval Flying Corps and had two other relatives holding commissions in the British Army.

The question of Dr Andraea's loyalty was beyond doubt. After being reassured that certain measures were being taken, the deputation withdrew, apparently satisfied, with the course proposed to be pursued. It was rumoured that the Territorials were called out to afford protection, but this was not so. The presence of military in the streets was only the marching of the ordinary picket and had no connection with the demonstration. The time of the passing of the picket happened to coincide with the presence of the crowd of people in the streets.

On the very same page of this newspaper was a prominent advertisement for 'A. SCHWARZ and Sons, Watchmaker and Jewellers of Holywell'. A more Germanic-sounding name it would surely be difficult to find.

The 'rounding up' of 'aliens' in North Wales

The *North Wales Chronicle* of Friday, 23 October 1914

reported action being taken in relation to 'aliens' on the North Wales coast:

GERMAN ALIENS
WHOLESALE ARRESTS IN NORTH WALES
HOME OFFICE ACTION

On Wednesday morning came an announcement that the measures adopted by the Government hitherto for the detection and suppression of espionage were being considered in the light of later developments of the war, has been followed by action of a decisive character.

An order has been issued by the Home Office to the police, instructing them to arrest all Germans, Austrians or Hungarians, resident in their district, of military age and to hand them over to the military authorities. As an immediate consequence of this order the police in London and in provincial towns – notably Manchester and Reading – were busily engaged yesterday in the work of 'rounding up' enemy aliens.

On Wednesday, an order was issued to the police to take into custody all alien enemies of military age – between 17 and 45, resident in Bangor, who have not taken out papers of naturalisation. Supt Griffiths took immediate steps and by Wednesday night four persons who were within the category of the new order were housed at the police station. Two of them are Germans and two are Austrians. One of the Germans was engaged as a waiter and the other has married a Welsh young lady.

One of the Austrians claims that he is over 45 years of age and that the order therefore, does not apply to him. It is understood that the War Office have instructed the local police to remove those to whom the order applies to a detention camp to-day.

The following week's edition of Friday, 30 October 1914 had further information on the matter, including details of some of the arrested 'alien enemies':

LLANDUDNO

THIRTEEN IN ONE DAY

Considerable excitement was caused at Llandudno, on Thursday, when it became known that the police acting under the new order, were arresting all Germans and Austrians in the town who were of military age. The local police force received the order the previous night, and every German and Austrian coming within its category were under detention by eleven o'clock yesterday morning. They included men of all classes, among them being some tradesmen, but the bulk were made up of hotel employees. Their names are: George Boyer, Jesmond Boarding House, Craig-y-Don; Joseph Chlebourn, Quinton, Harcourt Road; Ignay Frederick Labl, Prince of Wales Hotel; Anton Roba, Thirlmere, Lloyd Street; Mathias Schofman, Grand Hotel; Josiam Spatt, do.; John Bohm, North Western Hotel; Frederick Thaices, King's Road; Frank Sigl, Greenfield House, Clifton Road; Robert Hempel, North Western Hotel; Fritz Koran, do.; Fritz, Imperial Hotel; and Charlie, Clarence Hotel.

The men were taken by the 9.40 train this morning to the concentration camp at Queensferry and were escorted by members of the local police force and six special constables, under the command of Sergeant Richards.

The story of Hannah Hohn
The first that the public heard of Hannah Hohn (nee Evans) and her 'plight' was the account which appeared in the *Flintshire Observer* of Thursday, 29 October 1914. Her

struggle was like that of many British-born wives with German husbands:

WELSH WOMAN'S PLIGHT
A COMPLICATED CASE

An extraordinarily complicated case came before the St Asaph Board of Guardians, when a young married woman applied for relief. It was stated that she was born at Holyhead and had spent the greater part of her life in the parish of Cefn, near St Asaph. She married, at Conway, a German subject named Hohn and had had two children by him and was expecting another. Her husband was now a prisoner of war at York. She had three brothers in the British Army, one of whom was wounded at the Battle of Mons. The Clerk said that through her marriage the woman was a German subject. He hoped, however, that the case would not trouble the Board long, as he was communicating with representatives of the Soldiers' and Sailors' Families Association, with a view to that body taking it up. It was decided that one of the relieving officers should attend a meeting to be held at Denbigh, for the consideration of the case.

Under the provisions of the 'British Nationality and Status of Aliens Act', swiftly enacted by the British government on 7 August 1914, British-born wives of 'alien' men became persona non grata – pariahs in their own country of birth. Most of them received their 'allowances' not from the British government or local relief funds, but from the German authorities via a third party!

The next time that Hannah Hohn was publicly heard of was in the *Flintshire Observer* of Thursday, 12 November 1914. Below can be seen an extract from it:

The St Asaph Board of Guardians recently had before them a case of a rather complicated nature arising out of the war. A young woman named Hannah Hohn, formerly Evans, appealed to the Board for relief, explaining that she was destitute as a result of her husband Peter Hohn, a German subject, having been made a prisoner of war. But for the last two years she had resided at Chapel-en-le-Frith, near Buxton, where her husband had been engaged as a bandsman.

It was stated that the woman, although now an enemy alien, had a settlement in the parish of Cefn, and it was decided to see what could be done for her. As a result of the publicity given to the case, various agencies have been at work on her behalf and the Board of Guardians have now been notified that the American Embassy in London, German branch, has secured for the woman a weekly subsistence of 14 shillings per week for the support of herself and her two children. A letter to the Rector of Cefn, asking him to undertake the disbursement of the money concluded as follows:

'If Mrs. Hohn is of German birth, she should apply at once to the Home Office for repatriation; and if she is without funds this Embassy will bear the cost of her return to Germany.'

The last part of the piece above is a total misunderstanding of Hannah Hohn's circumstances, and indeed those of many British-born wives of German husbands living in Britain during the First World War.

The vast majority of German husbands with British-born wives were initially interned as 'alien enemies', yet they had never maintained any connection with the military, being hotel workers, barbers and musicians in German bands. The latter were very popular in Britain until, of course, the outbreak of war. Many such German husbands had to all intents and purposes severed their ties with the Fatherland, making a permanent life for themselves in Britain. Most marriages between British women and German men had taken place in Britain years before the war began, when the two countries were on the friendliest of terms, especially in the higher echelons of society.

The Saturday, 6 January 1917 edition of the *Abergele and Pensarn Visitor* included a further story relating to Hannah Hohn, as well as a rather unkind headline. In the eyes of the British authorities and many of her fellow Britons, as she was married to a German man, she was not just an 'alien', but an 'enemy alien':

AN ENEMY ALIEN'S VISIT TO KINMEL CAMP

A rather pathetic 'alien enemy' case came before the bench at St Asaph Petty Sessions on Monday, over which Colonel H. R. Lloyd Howard presided. A woman named Hannah Hohn whose address was given as Groesffordd, Cefn Meriadog was charged with 'having as an alien enemy, assumed a certain other name other than that by which she was ordinarily known at the commencement of the War, and as an alien enemy entered a prohibited area at Kinmel Camp on November 27th'. Replying to the first charge she said that she was guilty of going to the camp in her name of Evans and in answer to the second charge she said she thought that she was within her rights in going to the Camp, as it was in her own district.

Superintendent A. E. Lindsay of Rhyl stated that the defendants name before marriage was Hannah Evans, who in February of 1910 had married a German named Peter Hohn, at Conway, and that her husband had been interned in this country since the outbreak of the War. She was therefore by reason of her marriage an alien enemy. Some time ago she went to Kinmel Camp in search of employment as an assistant in the wet bar of one of the Camp's canteens. As a result of an interview with the Manager at the Camp for Melins Limited, to whom she gave the name of Hannah Evans, she gained employment. She signed the receipts given for wages paid to her in the name of Hannah Evans. The Superintendent added that the defendant lived with her father, whose house was within half a mile of the boundary between Denbigh and Flintshire and also within easy walking distance of the Kinmel Camp.

The *North Wales Weekly News* of that same week also covered the story of Hannah Hohn's court appearance, but with some different details, for here Hannah Hohn was said to have alleged that cruelty by her husband Peter Hohn had occurred against her since their marriage, and that before the war began she was living apart from her husband, because of his cruelty, and that she did not intend to live with him again.

The outcome of the court appearance was that the chairman, Colonel Howard, C. B., said that they looked upon the case as a very hard one and they were going to dismiss it with a caution. They understood that the defendant had three brothers fighting for this country and that one of them had been wounded. The offence appeared to be of a purely technical nature.

The *Denbighshire Free Press* of Saturday, 6 January 1917 carried the same story, referring to Hannah Hohn as 'a good-looking woman'. It also added one further piece of information, in that Superintendent Lindsay had made a search of the defendant Hannah Hohn's home, looking for any evidence of an incriminating nature which might expose her as a security risk to the country. Superintendent Lindsay stated the following to the court: 'Nothing was found of a character prejudicial to the interests of the Nation.'

One might now think this to be the end of the story of Hannah Hohn and her children, but it was not. She most certainly was not a quitter. The *Denbighshire Free Press* of Saturday, 9 November 1918 reported the following:

A GERMAN'S WELSH-BORN WIFE AND THE ALIEN RESTRICTION ORDER

Hannah Hohn, Groesffordd, Marli, Cefn, admitted that, being an alien enemy by marriage, she, on October 21st, entered a prohibited area, the rural district of St Asaph, without a permit issued by the registration officer of the district. Supt Woollam said that the defendant's parents were Welsh and lived at Groesffordd, Marli. Defendant married a German at Llandudno and her husband was interned on the outbreak of war. She then worked in a steam laundry at Holyhead till work was slack and a few days before October 21st she asked witness for permission to return to Marli as she could not live on the 16 s. allowed her by the German Government. He referred her to the Chief Constable, who refused permission. Witness, Supt Woollam, informed her by letter, but she returned nevertheless, though she admitted having received the letter. The Chief Constable had instructed him to take proceedings, but he did not wish to press the case.

Defendant said that she did not realise that the letter came from the Chief Constable. She thought she had to deal with Supt Woollam.

Supt Woollam said that he believed that the Chief Constable refused permission on account of overcrowding. Her husband had been repatriated, and he believed had told his wife that he expected to be shot, as he had refused to fight for his country.

> *The Chairman said they would take a very lenient course*
> *and fined defendant 1 s.*

Hannah Hohn (nee Evans) was born in 1884 at Holyhead, North Wales (some records show Llansannan, North Wales), and she first met Peter Hohn, who was born in 1880 in Bavaria, Germany, when they were both living and working in the North Wales seaside town of Llandudno in 1909. The couple were married at Llandudno in the Conway Registration District on 19 February 1910. At the time of their marriage, Hannah Evans was residing at 8 Jubilee Street, Llanduno, and Peter Hohn nearby at 29 Jubilee Street. The couple's first child Reina Hohn was born in 1910.

The 1911 Census shows us that Hannah Hohn, her husband Peter Hohn, their daughter Reina, and Hannah's Denbigh-born mother, Hannah Evans (Senior), were residing at 17 Norfolk Street, Oxford. Peter Hohn is shown as being a musician in a German band, and the family shared the property with four other German-born members of it.

Peter and Hannah Hohn's second child, Alvina Blanche Sarah Hohn, was born in 1912 at Oxford. A third child, Mair Hohn, was born to Hannah Hohn in 1915, and she was almost certainly fathered by Peter Hohn. However, in 1920, Hannah Hohn gave birth to a fourth child, who she named Hannah, probably more after her mother than herself. Having examined the birth certificate of this child, on which Peter Hohn is named as the father, a question has come to light, for the account in the *Denbighshire Free Press* edition of Saturday, 9 November 1918 stated that husband Peter Hohn had been repatriated, in truth deported, back to his homeland of Germany.

The shabby treatment of British-born women like Hannah Hohn who were married to German husbands, or indeed of German-born women belonging to the working class who remained in Britain during the war, was not meted out as such to women in the upper echelons of British society, for they were treated very differently. This is clearly and to my mind rather disgracefully shown in the story of Mabel Anne Savile, the sister of a German general. Her story first broke publicly in November 1915, and an account of it appeared in the Friday, 3 December 1915 edition of the *Edinburgh Evening News*:

GERMAN WOMAN IN WAR OFFICE
SISTER OF ENEMY GENERAL

Further questions will be asked in Parliament about Mrs Savile, a German by birth now employed in the War Office. She is the wife of the rector of Beverley, Yorkshire, which being 13 miles distant from the coast is within a prohibited area for enemy aliens. Questioned on the point already raised by Mr Joynson-Hicks, Mr Tennant, under-secretary of war replied; 'May I say that the wife of a rector in the Church of England who has shown she is thoroughly loyal to the country of her adoption is a person one can trust.' Mr Joynson-Hicks stated yesterday that he did not know Mrs Savile and he had no feelings at all in the matter. He was simply concerned with the question of principle. Whether it was a proper thing that the sister of a German officer fighting against us should be employed in the War Office. She is employed in the branch which deals with the distribution of the effects of dead soldiers. It is stated that her eldest daughter is similarly employed. The daughter is engaged to be married to Mr Everard Noel Rye Trantham, of the War Office.

A dark, handsome woman in the prime of her life, and a gifted conversationalist, Mrs Savile is described by those who have come into contact with her as possessing great personal charm. Her father was German and her mother English. She came here when she was four years of age. At their Beverley home Mr and Mrs Savile entertained some of the wife's relatives and among the guests it was said was one of the sons of Admiral von Tirpitz. That was before the war, but when war came tongues in Beverley began to wag. Mrs Savile was assured of the sympathies of many, but could not fail to be conscious that there was a section in the town who were suspicious and hostile. It was suggested that she had correspondence with her brother – General von Bothmer – who was in the German Army. The rectory was visited and searched, and eventually as Beverley came within the prohibited area around the Humber, Mrs Savile was informed by the military authorities that she had better leave.

Early this year Mrs Savile and Miss Savile came to London. On arriving in London Mrs Savile sought occupation and accepted in June, the appointment she now holds.

Unlike the three brothers of Hannah Hohn (nee Evans), Mabel Anne Savile's brother was not fighting in the British Army against Germany and the Central Powers, but fighting against Britain and its Allies in a high-level military capacity, for Mrs Savile's brother was General Count Felix von Bothmer (1852-1937), who was post-war ranked by leading military historians to be the eighth greatest German general of the First World War. He commanded the 6th Bavarian Division at Ypres early in the war, and then commanded in the Summer of 1916 in the fight against the Russians in the Brusilov Offensive. He was the recipient of many German military awards and decorations.

Mabel Anne Savile (nee Bothmer) was a daughter of

Count Hippolyt Viktor Alexander von Bothmer, and she married the Reverend William Hale Savile. I have found some accounts where Mrs Savile herself is referred to as '*Grafin* [in English: Countess] Mabel Anne von Bothmer Savile'. This means that a German-born sister and a British-born niece of an active enemy general were both working in the war office in London during the First World War!

More German hotel proprietors

The *North Wales Chronicle* of Friday, 30 October 1914 had two accounts of deeply felt anti-German sentiments, one being of the authorities taking action against an 'alien subject' from Betws-y-Coed, and the other being of 'a mob' marching from Llanrwst to Trefriw to remove an 'alien subject' themselves!

> *Two men in civilian clothes called at the Waterloo Hotel, Betws-y-Coed, on Thursday evening and had a short conversation with the German proprietor, Mr A. B. Theil, formerly of the Grand Hotel, Manchester, who is alleged to be a German officer, with the result that they all left together in a motor car, en route for Conwy. It subsequently transpired that Mr Theil had been interned for safety. In passing, it may be said that Mrs McCullock, the former owner of the valuable property, has again become the proprietor and proposes resuming her duties as hostess.*
>
> *About the same time a waiter engaged at the Belle Vue passed through a similar experience.*

The German proprietor of the Waterloo Hotel at Betws-y-Coed taken away for internment as an 'enemy alien' was Albin Huldreich Bruno Theil, born in Germany in 1878 to Edward Theil, a station master. In 1905, in Manchester, Albin Theil married Madge Wroe Embury, who was born at

44629. BETTWS -Y-COED: WATERLOO HOTEL.

The Waterloo Hotel, Betws-y-coed

Longport in Staffordshire, and they went on to have two children together: Edward Albin Theil, born 1907, and Robert Edgar Theil, born 1910. In 1911, Albin was the manager of the large and prestigious Grand Hotel in Manchester, residing there with wife Madge. They likely moved to the Waterloo Hotel at Betws-y-Coed so that Albin could own a hotel rather than simply manage one.

A brother of Madge Theil, William Hartley Wroe Embury, was a military-medal winner killed in action on 21 March 1917, aged thirty-two. He had been a bombardier, Service Number 56673, with 'B' Battery, 70th Brigade of the Royal Field Artillery. He died while fighting around Arras and is buried in Grave Reference 11.J.20, Faubourg D'Amiens Cemetery, Arras, Pas de Calais, France.

Whatever the exact fate of Albin as an internee during the First World War, he was most likely sent to the Isle of Man as a civilian internee, and by the 1920s, he once again lived on the British mainland with wife Madge.

At the time of Albin Bruno's death, aged sixty, on 13

December 1938, Albin and Madge were the proprietors of a restaurant at 551 Lordship Lane, East Dulwich, London. Albin died at the Royal Free Hospital, Gray's Inn Road, London. Probate of his estate went to his widow, Madge Wroe Theil.

If Albin Theil had lived for another year, he would have probably faced some more of the same 'anti-German fervour' that he had faced in Betws-y-Coed in late 1914, though I believe he had become a naturalised British citizen in 1928.

The article below relates to the fullest eye-witness accounts of a most serious occurrence, once again involving a German-born hotelier, and this time the appearance of 'a mob' who sought to remove the 'alien' from their midst, by force if necessary, and refusing to take 'no' for an answer!

GERMAN 'HUNT' IN CONWAY VALLEY
LLANRWST 'EXPEDITIONARY FORCE' INVADES
TREFRIW
PUBLIC PROTEST AGAINST INACTION OF THE
AUTHORITIES
REMARKABLE DEMONSTRATION AT TREFRIW
ULTIMATUM TO AN ALIEN
(From a Welsh Pioneer reporter)

On Friday morning, it was reported at Llanrwst that a public meeting would be held in Ancaster Square, in the evening, for the purpose of protesting against other Germans being allowed in the district.

About 7.15 p.m. groups of men began to gather on the square and by 7.30 p.m. several hundred men and women had assembled, when Councillor Albert Hughes, vice-chairman of the council, mounted the town hall steps and addressed the crowd. He said that every right-minded resident in the town felt it was their duty 'to clear every vestige of the enemy out of the district' (applause). It was true the authorities interned men up to the age of 45, but they ignored the fact that elder men were at least equally dangerous (applause). As long as a German was left in the valley they were unsafe and to allow one to remain would be an everlasting disgrace to them as a community (loud cheers). It did not matter what attitude these men assumed, they were always Huns at heart (applause). Although the authorities had been sweeping the countryside of these people there was one still left at the Belle Vue Hotel (hooting). He suggested that those present should form themselves into a peaceful procession, march to Trefriw and lodge an ultimatum with Mr Gipprich, that he must leave the district in a few days or take the consequences attending a refusal (loud applause). He urged upon all present however, to act peacefully and not to do anything contrary to the law (applause).

A crowd, estimated at about 250 strong, then formed into military order and marched down Station Road singing, 'It's a long way to Tipperary' and patriotic songs. On arriving at Gower's Bridge Tollgates, the crowd stopped, but in a few seconds the gates were thrown open and the 'expeditionary force' marched through free. Having negotiated the bridge safely they crossed the Carnarvonshire border to the strains of 'Rule, Britannia!'. The force, in spite of the darkness, marched along the Gower Road, a mile in length at a terrific rate and so closely packed where they that those in the rear ranks continually kicked the legs of those in front, with the result that the remarks passing between the 'warriors' were distinctly personal. As the force emerged from the darkness into the lights of the Trefriw public lamps, the National Anthem swelled out in volume, bringing the 'Spa folk' to their doorways in a rush. Here the force was reinforced by a

squad of Trefriw men and they fell into the 'goose step' past
the village hall to the hotel.

In the dark entrance to the hotel grounds were two silent
forms blocking the way. Owing to the dark, the 'Roosters' at
first thought they were German Uhlans but on closer
inspection, it was discovered that they were mere police
constables guarding the premises from the attack of the
invaders. At the request of Councillor A. Hughes, the 'force'
occupied a 'strategic position' on the main road and confined
itself to a vocal demonstration, whilst a deputation
consisting of Councillor A. Hughes, Messrs J. Smith
Williams and Jack Hughes, accompanied by the Pioneer
reporter as a war correspondent, penetrated the defences and
entered the premises. In the hall, they were met by a startled-
looking maid, who informed Councillor Hughes that Mr
Gipprich was dining. At the request of the deputation
however, she went to inform the manager of the honour
awaiting him. Mr Emil Gipprich immediately abandoned
his meal, and surrounded by the lady staff, confronted the
invaders' deputation…

Councillor Albert Hughes politely introduced himself
and his companions and explained that at a public meeting,
held at Llanrwst that evening, it had been resolved to clear
the district of German and Austrian aliens and that they
were appointed as a deputation to wait upon him to request
him to leave the district quietly and peacefully. Mr Hughes
added that Mr Gipprich's common sense would no doubt
lead him to look at his position in the proper light and that
as a result would leave the district without any necessary
delay.

Mr Gipprich replied that he had been informed of the
meeting and of the pending demonstration and had
communicated with his directors.

Mr A. Hughes: 'Who are they?'

Mr Gipprich: 'They live in London.'

Mr A Hughes: 'Their names please?'

Mr Gipprich: 'They will probably be here tomorrow.'

Mr A. Hughes: 'Will you give us the secretary's name?'

Mr Gipprich: 'Yes, Mr W. F. Goodwin, 67, Abbey Road, St John's Wood, London.'

Mr Jack Hughes: 'Are the mortgagees still in possession?'

Mr Gipprich: 'No, certainly not, the hotel is the property of the company.'

Mr A. Hughes: 'Of course we feel for you.'

Mr Gipprich: 'I doubt it.'

Mr A. Hughes: 'And we admit your position is a trying one.'

Mr Gipprich: 'What has it to do with Llanrwst?'

Mr A. Hughes: 'You reside in our district and as you are an enemy, we object to your presence here.'

Mr Gipprich: 'I have been here over 41 years and 31 years ago married an English lady. I am as loyal as you are. Moreover, this is not a matter for individual interference, but one for the authorities to deal with.'

Mr A. Hughes: 'Your age saves you from their attention, but we are determined you must go.'

Mr Gipprich: 'What good will that do to you?'

Mr A. Hughes; 'It will prevent a breach of the peace. I understand you are in the habit of visiting Germany every year.'

Mr Gipprich: 'I do certainly go there. When the war began I consulted my directors who asked me to stay here. I have been in two hostile countries already, as I was in Belgium in 1871, and I know what it is. I am loyal to this country, where my interests are. I can assure you that until I am relieved by the directors I will defend their property.'

Mr Jack Hughes: 'We represent hundreds of men, who are waiting outside.'

Mr Gipprich: 'I had heard of this and have taken the

necessary precautions, but I cannot give you an answer until I have consulted my directors.'

Mr A. Hughes: *'Well you must act quickly.'*

Mr Gipprich: *'Why?'*

Mr A. Hughes: *'Because we will not allow a representative of a nation which has committed such atrocities as the Germans to foul this fair valley by his presence.'*

Mr Gipprich: *'Am I responsible for the actions of the German Army?'*

Mr A. Hughes: *'You are a German and at heart sympathise with all their actions.'*

Mr Gipprich: *'I left Germany when I was 14 and went to Belgium, where I was educated then came to England.'*

Mr Jack Hughes: *'And you hope to die in Germany?'*

Mr Gipprich: *'I entertain no such wish, as my interests and associations are in this country and I will defend this hotel to the death.'*

Mr A. Hughes: *'Are you a naturalised British Subject?'*

Mr Gipprich; *'No.'*

Mr A Hughes: *'Why not?'*

Mr Gipprich: *'I was badly advised by my solicitor.'*

Mr A. Hughes remarked as the deputation left the hotel, that he hoped Mr Gipprich would accept the inevitable and leave the district or the responsibility would rest upon his own shoulders.

As the deputation appeared outside the hotel grounds their faithful followers raised a great cry of welcome and loudly demanded the result of the interview, but Mr A. Hughes ordered a march to 'The Shop' where he would address them. The 'British force' having assembled, Mr Hughes thanked them for the restraint they had exhibited, as they had on that occasion marched on a peaceful mission, but they were all determined to dig out every German that had taken ground in the district (applause). In a very short *time the German language in Wales would be included among the 'dead'; he only wished that every German was dead (great cheering). Mr Gipprich (hooting) had received the deputation courteously and was told it was the wish of the district that he should make himself conspicuous by his absence (applause). Mr Gipprich contended that he was a loyal member of the community, but the fact that he was a German contradicted that contention (applause). They had been informed that even one of the Ministers of the Crown employed a German (cries of – 'shame'), – but the time had come to purge the country of this poisonous bacillus (great cheering). These men, although deceitful, were full of tact and were able to disguise their real feelings, so the sooner they were sent away the better (applause). Mr Gipprich was in communication with his directors and unless he was able to furnish a favourable reply, another meeting would be held at Llanrwst, when measures would be adopted to force Mr Gipprich to obey the mandate of the people (loud cheering).*

The 'force' depleted of the Trefriw contingent, then marched back to Llanrwst, cheering and singing their war songs.

Mr Gipprich has since been arrested and taken to a concentration camp.

The German in question was Charles August Emile Gipprich. Born 22 February 1858 in Dortmund, Germany, he was a son of Bartholomaus Hubert Joseph Gipprich and Margaret Gipprich (nee Fenger).

In 1881, in the Liverpool Registration District, Charles August Emil Gipprich, known to most as 'Emil Gipprich', married Liverpool-born Annie Murphy. By 1891, Emil Gipprich was a commission agent living on Church Road, Hoose, West Kirby, Wirral, with his wife Annie and mother-in-law Annie Murphy (Senior), as well as a number of other relatives, including a sister-in-law and several nieces and nephews of his Gipprich family.

In 1901, Emil Gipprich was still a commission agent, but he and wife Annie were now residing on Banks Road, Hoylake, Wirral. Living with them was their eighteen-year-old son Edward and fifteen-year-old daughter Annie, both of whom were students. Also residing at the property was a niece by the name of 'Eleanor Jones', who was an organist by profession; and a young domestic servant named 'Margaret Rigby'.

By 1911, Emil Gipprich, aged fifty-three, was the hotel manager of the Belle Vue Hotel, Trefriw, in the Conway Valley, North Wales. His wife Annie, aged forty-eight, was the housekeeper of the hotel. Residing with them was a young book-keeper for the hotel named 'Annie K. Bestwick', two chambermaids, one kitchen maid, one scullery maid, and a fifteen-year-old boy from Pwllheli who looked after the boats. On the 1911 Census record, the Belle Vue Hotel had four paying boarding guests.

The Belle Vue Hotel at the time was a popular tourist haunt for paddle steamers operating between Conwy and Trefriw, and it allowed for passengers to disembark at Trefriw Quay, which was just over the road from the hotel. The establishment is still in business today, though it is now named 'The Princes Arms Hotel'.

Although Emil Gipprich was interned a few days after his tense confrontation with the 'angry mob' on the road outside the hotel premises, he was to be one of the truly lucky German internees. I write this because, unlike so many of his fellow 'alien internees', he and his wife Annie managed to be accepted into the then neutral United States.

On 1 May 1915, on the SS St Louis, Emil and Annie Gipprich departed from Liverpool Port, bound for a new life in the United States. They arrived on 10 May 1915 and began a new chapter in their lives. They went straight to Altoona, Pennsylvania, where Emil's brother Maximilian had been residing for some time at Number 323, 22nd Street. Indeed, Emil Gipprich had paid a six-month visit to his brother some years prior. Wife Annie had never been to the United States before, and as she was married to Emil, a German national, she was classed as also being a German national, though born and bred in Liverpool, England, and of British-born parents!

In Altoona, Emil Gipprich became the manager of the Junior Reform Club, which was affiliated to the Colonial Hotel and the Elks Lodge. Then, in 1920, the Gipprich family moved to reside in Riverside, Chicago, Illinois. Emil Gipprich now worked as a steward in a Chicago hotel until his retirement in 1931. It is rather strange to think that Emil and Annie Gipprich, formerly of the Belle Vue Hotel in Trefriw, a 'peaceful' Welsh village, found themselves living in Chicago in the Prohibition Era, sharing the streets with such notorious gangsters as Al Capone and Bugs Moran.

Emil Gipprich died aged seventy-seven (seventy-six, according to US official records) on 25 December 1935, and he was buried on 29 December 1935 in Saint Boniface Catholic Cemetery on North Clark Street in Chicago, Illinois. This cemetery was the first German cemetery in Chicago, and it contains the burials of many of the builders of the German Catholic community in Chicago, from when it was opened in 1863. At the time of Emil's death, his home address was given as 808 Crescent Place, Chicago.

Annie Gipprich survived her husband, and she died in 1940, also in Chicago, Illinois, aged seventy-six.

Financial assistance for 'alien enemies'
The *Flintshire Observer* of Thursday, 5 November 1914 had this:

RELIEF FOR ALIEN ENEMIES' WIVES

Several alien enemies at Bangor have been recently interned, leaving behind them wives of Welsh and English nationality. The Bangor War Emergency Relief Committee has resolved that these women should be relieved according to the dictates of humanity, and not according to the nationality thrust upon them by marriage with alien enemies.

An anti-German demonstration in Capel Curig

The *North Wales Chronicle* newspaper had the below account of an anti-German demonstration at Capel Curig, North Wales, in their Friday, 6 November 1914 edition:

ANTI-GERMAN DEMONSTRATION AT
CAPEL CURIG
ALIEN HOTEL PROPRIETOR REQUESTED TO
QUIT

The German proprietor of the Royal Hotel was the subject of a hostile demonstration on Friday evening. A considerable number of men and women assembled in the village and marched to the hotel. Three delegates entered the premises and requested an interview with Mr Baushoff. The manageress informed them that he was not on the premises. Eventually however they succeeded in getting into touch with him on the telephone. Mr Baushoff assumed a somewhat defiant attitude when told he must leave the district, naturally contending that it was a subject for the authorities and not an unauthorised mob. He was however informed that unless he had left the district by Monday evening the parishioners would take the law into their own hands and move him themselves. One of the female employees, a robust, muscular person, emerged from the hotel with her sleeves

The Royal Hotel, Capel Curig

rolled up to her shoulders and announced that she would assist the demonstrators to shift her German employer. The crowd, having indulged in a hostile vocal demonstration, dispersed.

The *Evening Telegraph* of Tuesday, 10 November 1914, had this sad story of a 'civilian casualty' of the ongoing war:

IRON CROSS FOUND IN POCKET
German Merchant Drowned

After attending at the Police and other offices at Denbigh, Ludwick Alexander Grossmann, a German residing at Glan y Wern Hall, disappeared and his body was discovered in the River Clwyd. Grossmann had resided for several years at Birkenhead, where he had conducted business as a rubber merchant.

The evidence at the inquest showed that he was greatly attached to Germany and Britain, and that the war had evidently preyed on his mind.

When his body was recovered an 'Iron Cross' was found in his pocket pointing to the fact that he took part in the war of 1870.

A verdict of 'found drowned' was returned.

Ludwick Alexander Grossmann, born in Germany in 1854, had carried out the business of a rubber merchant in Liverpool for some twenty-five years. For many of them, he had resided with his family at 'Zeelandia', Palm Grove, Claughton, Birkenhead. He had been fortunate to keep a wide circle of friends, being a member of the Birkenhead Arts Club, and was known to have given fine support to the inauguration of the local art gallery by contributing several paintings. He had also been a member of the Birkenhead Literary and Scientific Society.

A friend of Ludwick Grossman, Dr Harrington of Woodchurch Road, Birkenhead, gave evidence of identification and told the coroner's court that he had been staying as a guest at the deceased's home for a few days. He had been with the deceased on the morning of 7 November 1914, when the deceased stated that he was going out for a walk, but he did not return home for lunch, and in the late afternoon a search party scoured the area without locating him.

Mr Grossman's son would find some of his father's clothing near a riverbank not far from Glan y Wern Hall, Llandyrnog, near Denbigh. The following morning of 8 November 1914 the search for Mr Grossmann continued, and at about 11.30 a.m. his body was found in the river near Plas Ashpool Bridge, about one and a half miles downstream from where his personal items had been found the previous day. His head was protruding out of the water because an arm of the deceased was caught in the branch of a tree overhanging the river. When questioned, Dr Harrington stated that his friend had, to his knowledge, no domestic or business worries, but was deeply concerned about a personal matter.

Ludwick Grossman was deeply upset that England and Germany, the two countries he loved most, were at war. It also hurt him to know that, loving England as he did, he should be considered an 'alien enemy', for on the morning of 7 November 1914, he had been to Denbigh to try to take out naturalisation papers.

The Iron Cross found in Mr Grossmann's pocket, dated 1870, was from the Franco-Prussian War, when he would have been but sixteen years of age. So, this military medal may have been his, but more likely it was awarded to his father or another close male relative. No suicide note or similar was to be found anywhere.

Following the jury's verdict, they passed a vote of condolence to the widow and family of Mr Grossmann, with which the coroner associated himself.

Wives without required permits
The Thursday, 17 December 1914 edition of the *Flintshire Observer* had the article below, which concerns the wives of 'alien enemies' and the restrictions put upon their movements:

Alien Enemies Without Permits
First Cases of Kind in Flintshire
English Wives and Foreign Husbands

At the Hawarden Petty Sessions on Thursday, Paulina Loizka, a Hungarian living at Stockport, was summonsed for being an alien enemy travelling from Stockport to Queensferry without having obtained permission.

Superintendent Yarnell Davies said that this was the first case of its kind in Flintshire. Defendant was registered in the County Borough of Stockport, and her husband was a prisoner interned at the Queensferry Detention Barracks. On 12th November, Police Constable Thomas met the defendant in Chemistry Lane which led to the detention barracks, and asked her for her travelling permit, which she failed to produce. She was with a relative and said she had come to see her husband. He did not think Mrs Loizka would have had any difficulty in getting a permit to travel from the police at Stockport. She also stated she had not obtained a permit to travel because she did not know she ought to have had one. She was unable to see her husband owing to the fact she had not obtained permission to do so from the Commandant at the detention barracks. Defendant thought the restrictions only applied to men. Her husband was employed by a firm at Stockport and efforts were being made to secure his release. The secretary of the firm by whom defendant's husband was employed, said that the firm was thoroughly English, with every director and shareholder being Englishmen. No Germans or Austrians were connected with the company in any way. Mr Loizka was brought from Austria by the company as an oil specialist, and his place could not be filled by an Englishman because of the experience Mr Loizka had had in the oil fields of Austria. The chairman said the bench would let the defendant off, but warned her not to travel again without permission.

Williamina Heitman of Bootle, wife of a German interned at Queensferry, was summonsed for a similar offence. Superintendent Davies stated that on 10th November the defendant was found in Chemistry Lane and on being asked by the constable for her permit to travel, she failed to produce one. The constable ascertained that she was an English-born subject, but was married to a German. He believed some time ago she had made an application for a *travelling permit, but was refused one. The defendant said she obtained a permit from the Commandant at Queensferry to see her husband, and she thought that was sufficient. Her husband was employed as a tanner at Litherland, Liverpool, and had been at Queensferry for thirteen weeks. He was 34-years-old and had been in this country since he was three and a half. She had only been married eleven months and was now receiving 8 shillings a week from the Guardians. The bench asked the superintendent to suggest to the commandant at Queensferry that a footnote should be placed on the permit sent, stating that aliens must obtain a travelling permit to go for a distance of over five miles. They would let the defendant off this time, but she must not come again to visit her husband without an order from the police.*

Williamina Heitman (nee Cunningham) was born on 22 July 1884 in Everton, Liverpool. Her father was William Cunningham, a Liverpool-born lamplighter. For a number of years this Cunningham family resided in Toxteth Park, Liverpool.

Williamina had married Henry Heitman in the March quarter of 1914. On 15 October 1916, Williamina Heitman arrived at New York on the ship the *St Paul*. I am unable to ascertain whether her husband Henry Heitman was with her at this time. I have found that on 6 August 1927, Williamina and son Herman(n), aged five, left Liverpool on the White Star Line's passenger liner, the *SS Baltic*, once again bound for New York. Williamina, aged forty-three had given her occupation as housewife, and the address she gave on the passenger list was 39 Prior Street, Bootle, Liverpool. On this same list, it stated that the Heitmans intended to stay in the United States, and not to return to Britain. Williamina Heitman died in the United States in 1938, aged fifty-four.

Sadly, not every British-born woman married to a German during the First World War was treated as leniently by the courts as Williamina Heitman. For one young lady, it was a choice between paying a very hefty fine or going to prison. The *Llais Llafur* newspaper of Saturday, 24 July 1915 had this on the matter:

PLIGHT OF A GERMAN'S ENGLISH WIFE

Having married a German master tailor on the day before war broke out, Grace Mary Jungk, a good-looking young Englishwoman, was fined £5 or a month's imprisonment for having entered the prohibited area of Gravesend.

Her husband, she told the court, was interned a fortnight ago, and she had been unable to procure work. She had lately been living at Twickenham. Every position she obtained, she was dismissed from on account of her married name. Finding it impossible to live in London, she came to her English parents at Gravesend.

The prisoner declared that her parents could not pay the fine, and she elected to go to prison.

It was being considered in mid-1915 that the German-born women in Britain should also be interned for the duration of the war as 'enemy aliens', as was already happening to German men. Also, the lives of British-born women married to German men in Britain were proving very difficult. *The Times* edition of Thursday, 13 May 1915 had an interesting article on such matters, written from a female perspective:

GERMAN WOMEN IN LONDON
BRITISH WIVES OF ALIENS
(From A Woman Correspondent)

The question of the internment of German women was stated yesterday at Scotland Yard to be under consideration. At the Home Office the authorities said it was a matter for the War Office, and at the War Office it was stated to be a matter for the Home Office.

Meanwhile the German women in London regard the idea with horror. They are asking where will the room be found for them – they number many thousands – if the housing problem has proved a difficulty in the case of their interned husbands. Nearly all the single women have been repatriated or have gone with Home Office permits – obtained with great difficulty – to the United States. Many have definitely refused repatriation, having left home through some family quarrel, and not lived there for many years. When war broke out there was a large number of German women – clerks, typists, commercial travellers, students and tourists in London, but those with few exceptions have been repatriated. The women who are here now are mainly the British or German wives of German men who have been interned, or are middle-aged and elderly German women who have lived here for so long that they have lost touch with their own country. Their sympathies are, however German, and they make no attempt to conceal the fact, though German women of the better-classes avoid all allusion to the war when in the company of English people.

THE SERVANT QUESTION

Work is made absolutely impossible for them with one curious exception – the German cook, whose position has fluctuated since war broke out. In the largest of the servant' agencies it was stated yesterday that German servants had been dismissed almost everywhere and that the German cook was rare in English families. In one of the German women's associations, on the contrary, it was said that though German servants were dismissed at the beginning of the war, many applications were afterwards received from English women overwhelmed by the servant difficulty of German cooks. These are perhaps the only German women employees in Britain.

There has been a considerable amount of suffering among German women and British women married to Germans since the war. Only eleven per cent of the German men at large are in employment and there is much poverty. The German Government through American intermediaries make an allowance paid through the German Benevolent Society at 10 shillings a week, and 3 shillings a week for each child to the wives of interned Germans. While the British Government make a grant paid through the Relieving Officer of 8 shillings outside the London radius, and 10 shillings inside, and 1s 6d for each child to the English wives of interned Germans. Where 6 shillings or more has to be paid for rent and the children require much milk the allowance does not go far. The mental distress of those who have male relatives fighting in Germany and who have been frightened by the occurrences of the last couple of days, feeling is so strong that anyone with a German name is treated with suspicion. A distinguished English woman archaeologist whose family have been resident over 80 years here, can obtain work nowhere because she has a German name. The Friends Emergency Committee for the Assistance of Austrians, Germans and Hungarians in distress have dealt with over 3,000 cases.

An official announcement on 'aliens' from the British government was printed in many newspapers, including the Friday, 14 May 1915 edition of the *North Wales Chronicle*:

ALIENS TO BE INTERNED
GOVERNMENT DECISION

The Government's scheme for dealing with the 40,000 hostile aliens now at large in the United Kingdom was announced by Mr Asquith in the House of Commons yesterday. The outlines of the scheme are as follows:

Men of Military age to be interned. Men over Military age, all to be repatriated. Women and children to be repatriated, and in some cases to be allowed to remain. Applications for exemption to be dealt with by an advisory body.

A 'Letter to the Editor', with somewhat sinister undertones, was published in the same edition of the *North Wales Chronicle*:

Sir,

Would it be possible for you to inform the public of Bangor whether or not it is a fact that two German women are on the staff, or have any connection with, the Bangor County School for Girls?

Reply from the Editor:

So far as our knowledge goes, the only persons who before the war bore names of apparently foreign origin – changed by legal process since the war broke out – were Miss Grunbaum and Miss Zimmerman.

Miss Grunbaum and Miss Zimmerman managed to change their clearly Germanic-sounding names to more British-sounding ones in the nick of time, for in 1916, a new law was brought in that 'enemy aliens' in Britain were now forbidden to change their names. In 1919, this ban was extended to all 'foreigners' residing in Britain, and it was only lifted in 1971.

In the following week's edition of Friday, 21 May 1915 was the following:

CORRESPONDENCE
ARE THERE GERMAN WOMEN IN BANGOR?
AN EXPLANATION.
(TO THE EDITOR)

Sir,

Regarding a letter in your last issue headed 'Are there German Women in Bangor?' As I have acted as Chairman of the Bangor County School for Girls since Professor Milner Barry left Bangor to join the Navy last autumn, perhaps I may be allowed to answer the question in so far as it is directed at that institution.

The answer is that there are no German women on the staff of the school. There are, it is true, two natural born British subjects, who at the outbreak of the war bore German names. In order to make clear the fact that they were British Subjects and British in sentiment and sympathy, early in the war and by the process of law, both changed their German names for the English equivalents.

I may add that brothers of both these ladies hold commissions in the British Army.

Yours, etc.
Reginald W. Phillips
2 Snowdon Villas,
Bangor.

From the Editor:

We are glad to publish this explanation as we have received several letters bearing upon the same matter, which under the circumstances we have not published.

Anti-German riot in Rhyl

Following the sinking of the passenger liner the *RMS Lusitania* by the German U-Boat *U-20* on 7 May 1915, resulting in the loss of 1,198 lives, anger was felt across the length and breadth of Britain, not least of all in the seaside resort of Rhyl in North Wales. It was two weeks later, on the evening of 21 May 1915, that a most strange character by the name of 'Arthur Robert Brougham', a piano tuner from the London area who was lodging in Rhyl, was caught shouting pro-German slogans on the Foryd Bridge. This would serve as the catalyst for what was to follow.

Brougham was taken to Rhyl police station and a group of men, including locally billeted soldiers, many the worse for drink, made their way to there with the intention of getting at him, whom they were loudly shouting was a 'German spy'. Unable to gain entrance into the police station and feeling somewhat frustrated, it was someone's idea, at about 9.15 p.m., that they should as one group make their way to Queen Street, where a known German man lived and ran a barber's shop and tobacconist business.

That German was Robert Fassy, who in 1912 had married a local woman, Edith Fassy (nee Gunner), whose family had for many years managed a successful boot and shoemaking business in the area. The Fassy family had at this time two small children, Jean, aged two; and Donald, aged six weeks.

By the time that the group of men were outside the premises of 35 Queen Street, they had well and truly become a riotous mob. Without thought, they began to smash the windows of the premises, above which the family resided and were at home. It is awful to think how absolutely petrified they must have been as the baying mob smashed their windows, stole all the items from the shopfront, and directed vile verbal abuse at them.

Robert Fassy, aged twenty-seven at the time, was born on the border between Germany and Switzerland, and had from 23 October 1914 to 25 October 1914 been interned as an 'enemy alien' at the Queensferry Detention Barracks. However, following certain sureties having been given on his behalf by a number of Rhyl business people, he was released and allowed to return home to his family. He had some years earlier served what he said was a compulsory one year of service in the German Army.

With the police in attendance, the Fassy family, carrying their small children were escorted through the 'baying and jostling mob' to the relative safety of the nearby police station, but not before the mob had tried to get at them and physically assaulted the police officers. Where the family went, the mob followed, and they broke five panes of glass while attempting to force their way inside the police station. It was clear they were totally out of control, and their numbers had by this time increased. An urgent call was made to Brigadier General Dunn at the nearby Kinmel Park Training Camp. He attended the scene promptly and with a military piquet got the soldiers in the mob to disperse and fall-in at nearby Bodfor Street. The remaining members of the mob, the civilians, slowly disappeared into the night.

The Fassy family's life truly changed forever. That night and the following one, they 'quietly' stayed at Edith Fassy's brother's house of 6 Victoria Avenue, Rhyl. Her brother, George William Gunner, had been wounded fighting for the British Army on the Western Front.

Soon after, the Fassy family left Rhyl for Birmingham, where they had some family connections. As far as I can ascertain, they never returned to their home and business premises of 35 Queen Street, Rhyl. The mob got their way and forced Robert Fassy and his family out for good.

Horatio Bottomley

The *North Wales Chronicle* of Friday, 11 June 1915 had the article below, which concerns the House of Commons and relates to a local MP suggesting where 'aliens still at large' could be interned:

> *KINMEL CAMP*
> *LOCAL M.P.'S QUESTIONS ABOUT ALIENS*
>
> *Colonel Walker is to ask the Home Secretary to-day, whether he will communicate with the Secretary for War with the object of taking over the encampment for 40,000 which has been erected in Kinmel Park, Abergele, so that immediate accommodation can be found for the aliens still at large.*

The *Flintshire Observer* of Thursday, 8 July 1915 reported upon more arrests of 'alien enemies':

> *ALIEN ENEMIES INTERNED*
> *Nine Germans and one Austrian removed from Flintshire*
>
> *On Monday last, Superintendent Davies of Mold and other police officers conveyed to the internment camp of Handforth, near Stockport, nine Germans and one Austrian, all of military age from the county of Flintshire.*

The *Flintshire Observer* newspaper of Thursday, 23 September 1915 contained this:

Hawarden Board of Guardians
The German's Wife

A discussion ensued on the question of relief for an interned German's wife, child and the wife's sister. It was decided to grant relief amounting to 15 shillings for the three.

Guaranteed not to calm things down in relation to any anti-German hatred in your locality, was having Horatio Bottomley (1860-1933) give one of his public addresses. Bottomley was the editor and proprietor of the *John Bull* periodical, in which he would 'vent his spleen' on anything and everything Germanic. Following the sinking of the *RMS Lusitania*, he wrote of Germans being 'unnatural freaks'. His excoriating anti-German remarks wound up his readership and his audiences, and on occasion matters got way beyond the reasonable. One such example is when Horatio Bottomley, in the 15 May 1915 edition of *John Bull*, unequivocally called for the extermination of all Germans in Britain, even those who were now naturalised British citizens. He even officially addressed the sailors of the British Grand Fleet at Scapa Flow on what was called a 'morale-boosting visit'. He also spoke at recruiting rallies around the country.

On 17 August 1915, Horatio Bottomley addressed a large paying audience at the Pavilion and Gardens Theatre, Rhyl, North Wales, on the subject of 'the present situation in the war'. On the previous evening at the same venue, the great music hall comedian George Robey, nicknamed 'The Prime Minister of Mirth' had performed.

Horatio Bottomley was a journalist, financier, newspaper editor and proprietor, and a twice-elected Member of Parliament. He was also a long-time and rather successful crook – a fraudster, what was often called a 'swindler'. He would spend money he did not have and raise money purportedly to be for good causes, but in fact it would end up in his grubby pockets. He was finally convicted by a court of law when caught issuing so-called 'victory bonds'. In 1922, he was found guilty and sentenced to seven years of imprisonment, of which he served five. He died in 1933, a broken husk of a man.

A strange and melancholic story

This strange and rather melancholic story appeared in the Friday, 7 January 1916 edition of the *North Wales Chronicle*:

A GERMAN'S WIFE IN KHAKI
SINGULAR EPISODE AT LLANRWST

Annie Leiser, the wife of an interned German, was sentenced to seven days of imprisonment by the Llanrwst Magistrates on Saturday for absconding from the union workhouse.

Mr J. T. Jones, the workhouse master, stated that the prisoner entered the house with her five children some months ago. A cousin of the prisoner residing in Liverpool had intimated her readiness to adopt one of the children and on Friday the defendant was granted two hours' leave from 2.30 p.m. to prepare for the child's removal. The woman failed to appear at the specified time and later in the evening he was informed that she was drunk and disorderly in Scotland Street. He reported the matter to the police.

Inspector E. Jones stated that when he arrested the prisoner at 12.15 that morning, in a house in Chapel Street, she was wearing a soldier's full uniform and trying to drill a lady friend whose evolutions, to say the least, were exceedingly erratic.

The defendant, who pleaded guilty, said she had nothing to say.

Frederick Leiser had been interned as an 'alien enemy' in October of 1914. His wife, Annie Leiser (nee Evans), was born in 1889 at Llanrwst. They had married in the September quarter of 1908 in Llanrwst.

In 1911, Frederick Leiser had been a pork butcher living at 5 Lloyd Terrace, Scotland Street, Llanrwst, with wife Annie and their children. In 1915, the Leisers had a fifth child they named William, born no doubt after Frederick Leiser was interned, thus leaving wife Annie to 'fend for herself'.

Annie Leiser died in the June quarter of 1934, in the Conway Registration District, aged forty-five. Frederick Leiser does not appear to have been repatriated or forcibly deported back to his native Germany, during or indeed after the First World War, as he died in the Hiraethog Registration District, in the September quarter of 1956, aged eighty-two, according to official records, though I believe his age at death was in fact seventy-six.

More on 'enemy aliens' not interned

In the Summer of 1916, not everyone was welcome to set up bathing facilities on the beach at Barmouth. The *North Wales Chronicle* of Friday, 18 August 1916 had the following:

BARMOUTH

The season is now full on and the town is very well patronised by visitors. Inspector Watkin Owen is now authorised to grant permits to erect bathing tents on the beach, to applicants who are not aliens.

Even into mid-1917, the 'alien enemies' in Britain who were at large and not interned were still an ongoing issue. The

North Wales Chronicle of Tuesday, 4 May 1917 had the following:

LLANDUDNO ALIEN TAILORS
QUESTION IN PARLIAMENT

Mr Joynson-Hicks in the House of Commons on Tuesday, asked the Home Secretary whether he had received a petition from the tailors of Llandudno and district pointing out that in Llandudno there were four tailoring establishments under the control of alien enemies, of whom two were interned after the outbreak of the war, but were subsequently released; whether he was aware that several English tailors had to close their businesses because they had joined the colours and that others would shortly do so; and whether the Government would take definite steps in regard to this case and others, to prevent the businesses of honest Britons being stolen by alien enemies.

Mr Brace: 'Yes, the petition has been received and enquiries have been made, which show that it is not the case that there are at the present time four tailoring establishments at Llandudno under the control of alien enemies. The only tailors of enemy nationality now in Llandudno are two Bohemian Czechs, who have been in this country for 21 and 15 years respectively, are married to British subjects, have a number of British-born children, and, though technically of enemy nationality are pro-Ally in their sympathies. They were interned for a short period at the commencement of the war, but were exempted from internment on the recommendation of the Advisory Committee. They are both anxious to enlist in the British Army and with this object in view have been before medical boards. If they are not accepted for the army they will be required to undertake work of national importance.'

The First World War was dragging on and approaching its fourth 'anniversary' when calls were made in the country for further restriction of 'enemy aliens'. The *Denbighshire Free Press* of Saturday, 6 July 1918 had this:

NORTH WALES AND ALIENS

The strong agitation in the country for internment of all Aliens has spread to North Wales. Bangor City Council have passed a resolution calling on the Government to intern every Alien of enemy origin; but Sir Henry Lewis protested against so wholesale a measure.

In the House of Commons last night, the Home Secretary said there were still un-interned Aliens in this country: 6,000 Germans, 5,500 Austrians, Turks or Bulgarians 1,100. Total – 12,600. Of these 4,000 are friendly race and only technically of enemy nationality. Czechs, Poles, Alsatians, and over 3,000 are old men or invalids. Of the 6,000 Germans, over 3,000 are married to British wives; over 4,000 have British born children and 2,400 have sons serving in the British forces.

The *North Wales Chronicle* of Friday, 2 August 1918 gave the 'alien' numbers for the county of Caernarfonshire:

CARNARVONSHIRE POLICE COMMITTEE
ALIENS IN THE COUNTY

Replying to a question by Mr J. R. Pritchard, the Chief Constable said there were not many aliens in the county. In fact, there was nothing to justify the alarmist rumours that were going about. In his opinion, the whole matter might have been left in the hands of the Home Secretary. In Caernarfonshire, there were only seven German-born males and three females; and twelve British-born females who were now of German nationality; of Austrians, there was one male and four British-born females. There were many hundreds of other aliens.

As late as September 1918, it was still being discussed at government level whether or not the British-born wives of German husbands who were living in Britain should be deported to Germany – a country the vast majority of the women had no connection with and had never been to! Their only connection was a husband who, though born in Germany, may not even himself have been there for many years, and was now interned in Britain for the duration of the war. *The Times* newspaper of Saturday, 14 September 1918 had this on the matter:

BRITISH BORN WIVES OF GERMANS
NO ENFORCED DEPORTATION
The following correspondence has passed between Sir Henry Dalziel, M.P., and Sir George Cave, the Home Secretary:

1 Portland Place, London, September 10.

Dear Sir George Cave,

You may have observed that a strong protest has been made in various influential organs of the Press against the alleged deportation to Germany of British wives of German husbands. The assumption is made that this is in some way the act of the Government, as the result of the more stringent measures that have been taken, following upon the report of the Advisory Committee, of which I had the honour to be chairman. As I am personally very strongly opposed – and I believe in this I am expressing the views of every member of my committee – to British-born women being forcibly sent to an enemy country, I should be glad to know whether the Home Office is in any way responsible for such a policy. I can hardly believe that it is so; but I await your reply with considerable interest.

– HENRY DALZIEL.

Home Office, September 12.

Dear Sir Henry Dalziel,

In reply to your letter of the 10th inst., there is no foundation for the suggestion that the British-born wives of German husbands are being deported to Germany against their will. Some four or five British-born women have been required to leave because they had shown themselves violently pro-German, some of these, though British-born, being of German origin; but with these negligible exceptions any British-born woman or child who has left the country for Germany, has done so voluntarily.

When a British-born woman applies to the Home Office for a permit to go to Germany, she is required to produce satisfactory evidence that some relative or friend in Germany is willing to receive and look after her and her children, and the hardships which she will probably have to endure in Germany are pointed out to her; and it is only when she persists in asking to be allowed to go that the permit is granted. British-born children over eight are not allowed to go until they have been separately interrogated and it is ascertained that they really wish to accompany their mother, and in no cases are British-born boys over 15 years of age permitted to go.

It is true that, in spite of these precautions, a considerable number of these women have elected to go to Germany and to take their young children with them, either because they desire to follow their deported husbands, or because being of German name and nationality, they have found that life here is made intolerable for them; but the Home Office cannot be held responsible for that result.

– GEORGE CAVE.

Germany's 'enemy aliens'

However harsh one might think the British authorities' internment of male 'alien enemies' during the First World War was, and regardless of what one might make of their lack of compassion for the British-born wives and children of husbands deemed 'alien enemies', these things pale in comparison with the German authorities' treatment of those they regarded as such.

In early 1915, some 4,273 British civilian men were interned at what was formerly a racecourse at Ruhleben, near Berlin. Though conditions were poor, it was nothing compared to what the Germans meted out to others, for as the war progressed, so did the utter cruelty of the German authorities towards two main groups of civilians; firstly, civilians who found themselves in their 'own countries' under German occupation, and secondly, the many thousands of migrant workers trapped inside Germany when the First World War broke out.

In countries the Germans occupied, such as Belgium, they ensured that those who opposed them would be executed or sent to internment camps like Holzminden, Rastatt and Havelberg. German atrocities against Belgian civilians did take place, of that there is no doubt whatsoever. For example, in October 1916, the Germans forcibly deported around 60,000 Belgian males to work as forced labour in Germany. A further 62,000 were forced to work in semi-military 'civil workers battalions' (in German: *zivil arbeiter bataillon*), which involved working behind the lines on the Western Front. Both of these groups of deported men worked under military discipline, were housed in camps, and were forced to wear red armbands which classed them as civilian prisoners. A few thousand of them (the exact figure is not known) did not survive the war.

At Easter in 1916, an estimated 20,000 French women and girls were despicably deported – the Germans euphemistically called it 'relocation' – from the industrial cities of Lille, Tourcoing and Roubaix in northern France, and forced to carry out agricultural work in other parts of German-occupied France. Many of these female civilians were dragged screaming from their families at the sharp end of a bayonet! They were made to undergo gynaecological examinations, and were said to have been treated like common prostitutes.

The German authorities, knowing that many, many thousands of foreign migrant workers were in Germany at the outbreak of war, issued certain decrees which meant that around 300,000 Russian-Pole seasonal agricultural workers (a small number in industrial work) were forbidden to leave Germany for their homeland, or to leave their German employers. They were therefore used as forced labour.

An estimated 300,000 men living in Russia, Poland or other Baltic State countries now under German occupation were 'forcibly recruited to work in Germany' itself, to aid the German war effort.

As for POWs, the worst treatment of all reserved by the Germans was for those who were Russian and Romanian, two nationalities treated as farm animals, not human beings. By comparison, the British internment of their 'aliens' was extremely mild, indeed benign, though not something to be proud of!

It was not just the warring nations like Britain and Germany who interned so-called 'civilian alien enemies'. Neutral countries such as the Netherlands also took part. They interned several different groups, including civilian refugees; deserters from the warring countries; escaped POWs; and what were referred to as 'unwanted guests', who were a mish-mash of persons who entered the Netherlands for reason(s) not fully known, and by doing so could well have put the country's neutrality at risk.

It is estimated that throughout Europe up to 800,000 civilians experienced internment.

Chapter Fourteen

Espionage?

'Spy fever'

During the First World War, under the 'Defence of the Realm Act', which was introduced in Britain on 8 August 1914, a total of eleven German spies were executed by firing squad in the Tower of London. The most famous of these was Carl Hans Lody, who used the alias of 'Charles A. Inglis'. Lody was a reserve officer of the Imperial German Navy, and during the Third Reich he would be resurrected as a symbol of German patriotism. The Nazis, in 1937, even named one of their new destroyers after him – the *Hans Lody*.

In truth, neither the German spy network in Britain nor the British spy network in Germany during the First World War were 'up to much', as they were both rather ad hoc entities. However, whilst there may not have been the

'Help to catch Huns' – a WWI postcard

thousands of German spies in Britain as conjured up by the British press and believed by most of the ordinary British public, far more existed than were ever caught. These German spies, real or imagined, resulted in quite a number of totally innocent British men being suspected, and on occasions, being wrongly arrested.

In wartime Britain, anyone with a foreign-sounding name, especially a Germanic one, immediately became a 'suspicious person', and this became even worse for them if they spoke with a foreign accent. In this febrile atmosphere, Germanaphobia and 'spy fever' abounded.

The German breed of dog known as 'the dachshund' was sometimes kicked, stoned or even poisoned in British streets because of its name and association with Germany. One highly popular cartoon advertisement for British victory bonds depicted a 'British Bobby' police officer in uniform carrying a rifle, dragging by the scruff of the neck a uniformed German soldier, with a reluctant dachshund being dragged behind on a lead, with the tagline, 'Help to Catch Huns'. Many postcards and cartoons of the time depicted the British bulldog with a Union Jack getting the better of a German dachshund in various ways. Even in the United States, dachshunds were being renamed to 'liberty pups' by many of their owners!

Everything in Britain, from foodstuffs to diseases with an obvious German or Germanic connotation, was renamed. The hamburger became a Salisbury steak; sauerkraut (from where, 1918 onwards, the derogatory term of 'kraut' came) became liberty cabbage; German measles became liberty measles, and so on.

This xenophobia was widespread among many, but we should not forget that such feelings were felt in Germany against the British – it was not a one-way street. Still, it must fairly be stated that the Germans only began interning

British civilians after Britain had started the practice against them first. On the other hand, it should be said that, at the outbreak of war, there were far more German, Austrian and Hungarian civilians in Britain than British civilians in these enemy countries.

Only a few days after the war began came the speedy enactment into law of the 'British Nationality and Status of Aliens Act'. Formerly innocuous hobbies and pastimes soon took on sinister overtones, especially when being carried out by those constituted to be not just 'aliens', but 'alien enemies'.

The *Flintshire Observer* of Thursday, 27 August 1914 had this:

CARRIER PIGEONS
ALIEN POSSESSORS SENT TO PRISON

Max Wilhelm Nagel, of Mornington Crescent, Regents's Park, dealer, and Charles King, dealer, Ashford Common, were charged jointly at Feltham, London, on Monday, with being in unlawful possession of sixty carrier pigeons, at Mount Pleasant, Ashford. Nagel was sent to prison for two months, and King, who admitted having fought against the British in South Africa, and who was also charged with failing to register as an alien, was sent to prison for six months.

Yes, the carrier pigeons may have been intended to be used by the two men for some subversive activity, but the fact that Charles King had fought against the British some thirteen years earlier in South Africa obviously had a bearing upon matters beyond what it should have done. It was clear that those who continued in wartime Britain to pursue hobbies and pastimes such as birdwatching, hiking, fossil hunting, and outdoor photography would come under suspicion, whether they be so called 'alien enemies' or not!

The *Flintshire Observer* of Thursday, 20 August 1914 carried the following intriguing story:

SPY OR ARTIST?
A Remarkable Story of a German with Camera and Pencil Sketches and Photographs

The calm and placid everyday life of Llanarmon, the prettily situated village just over the border in Denbighshire, has been disturbed for the past week or two by a somewhat remarkable story. Some time ago a German came to reside in the village and his amiability quickly made him well liked. Apparently, he was a man of artistic tastes and was fond of roaming the countryside with pencil and camera.

Eventually however ominous suggestions began to spread as to the reasons for these excursions. It was stated that the man had been seen making sketches – and in some cases, taking photographs – of places which the most vivid imagination could not conceive to be artistic.

In brief, it was pointed out that it was not unreasonable to suppose that this man's work with pencil and camera had a sordid and practical side – that the sketches and photographs were made for the German military authorities, who are known to expend money as lavishly as connoisseurs for this class of 'artistic' work. Any opportunity for putting to the test the truth or otherwise of these suspicions passed away, with the departure from the village a few weeks ago of the individual in question. About ten days ago, a man bearing a name exactly similar to that of the German who had been living at Llanarmon, was brought before a Sussex bench of magistrates on a charge of espionage.

The taking of holiday-type photographs in wartime North Wales was a hazardous proposition, as the *North Wales Chronicle* of Friday, 16 October 1914 informed its readers:

CONWAY
PHOTOGRAPHERS ARRESTED

Two gentlemen were on Tuesday, observed taking photographs of the Conway Bridge and the Castle. They were immediately arrested by the military guard and taken to the police station, where they gave a satisfactory explanation, stating that they were visitors from Sheffield, and were, therefore, released.

In the following month, a more humorous incident of a like nature occurred in the Conway Valley and was reported upon in the Friday, 13 November 1914 edition of the *North Wales Chronicle*:

MISTAKEN FOR A GERMAN
A GOVERNMENT OFFICIAL ARRESTED IN THE CONWAY VALLEY

One of the best known and most popular H.M. Inspectors of Schools, on Friday, met with an amusing adventure in the Conway Valley. It appears he was walking along some fields admiring the beautiful autumn tints of the foliage on the trees, when his delightful vision was rudely dispelled by a heavy hand laid upon his shoulder, and the gruff voice of a gamekeeper demanding, 'What do you want here? Don't you know you are trespassing?'

The Inspector, who is something of a humourist, immediately resolved to assume the character of a German, and fiercely replied, 'spretchau de dikes', whereupon the gamekeeper clutched him by the arm shouting, 'Come on you blooming German, we will see about your little game, you infernal Hun.'

Dragging his 'prisoner' along, the gamekeeper told him in

fluent terms what he thought of Germans in general, and his prisoner in particular, the Inspector occasionally interpreting a German command.

At last, finding the pace too hot, the Inspector turned quickly to his captor, and asked him in Welsh where they were going to.

The gamekeeper gasped and relinquished his grasp, and having regained the use of his suspended faculties enquired, 'Are you a Welshman?'

'Certainly', replied the Inspector and immediately divulged his identity. The gamekeeper was naturally profuse in his apologies.

The Inspector shortly afterwards arrived at Betws–y-Coed carrying a couple of rabbits, and wearing a satisfied smile!

The *Flintshire Observer* of Thursday, 26 November 1914 carried this very personal advertisement of an unusual nature:

£50 REWARD

NOTICE IS HEREBY GIVEN that the sum of £50 will be paid to anyone whose evidence would lead to a conviction of the person or persons who have falsely and maliciously circulated a report to the effect that I, W. G. Richardson, Central Buildings, Buckley (branches Hawarden and Mold), am a German or other alien. Information to be forwarded to Messrs Keene and Kelly, Solicitors, Mold.

Suspected German spies and agents in North Wales were apparently everywhere, even on the tops of mountains, as the *Flintshire Observer* of Thursday, 6 May 1915 related:

'GERMHUNITIS'

The mountain ranges through the length of this county, have frequently since war broke out been alleged to be the resort of suspicious persons intent upon map-studying and signalling. The stories of strange men and even strange women making inquiry of country people – of their being seen by the hour in some sheltered nook, with a command of the sea in front of them – have been told with much circumstantial force.

So much has the spy scare grown and expanded in the minds of inhabitants, that they eye with suspicion, anyone who does not carry his business and his purpose 'on his sleeve' as it were.

The other day the inhabitants of one of the sequestered mountain villages had the time of their lives – they imagined that a real live actual 'spy' was in their midst. An elderly man with a grey beard trimmed to a sharp point came unannounced to the village. He sought accommodation, wanting to stay a short while just for a quiet restful holiday from the hustle and stress of business in a city by the sea.

The second chapter in this story has for its setting the fossil-laden heaps of stone that abound on the hills. With a hammer and a chisel, he tapped and smashed at the rock. Then he was seen consulting a map. He was watched and stalked and at last some men in the village decided 'to see what he was up to'. He was subjected to a running fire of interrogatories.

The slip of painted pasteboard which he produced, his personal letters and other documentary evidence, failed to convince them of his identity and that he was merely a visitor.

Down towards the village the visitor was escorted, hedged in by the doughty village men and with a screen of young hopefuls tripping over gorse and heather. Further *investigation of his credentials was made and for a time he was held in durance. City references were given and telephonic confirmation was sought.*

At last, as a result of the inquiries, everything was found satisfactory and thus terminated the adventure which had disturbed his peaceful hunt for fossils.

It can be presumed that the 'Letter to the Editor' below, first published in Flintshire's *County Herald* newspaper of Saturday, 15 May 1915, was from the same 'suspected spy', and not from another poor unfortunate:

THE SPY AND SUSPICION PERILS

Dear Sir,

May I through the medium of your valuable paper ask 'the powers to be' to issue some instructions for the guidance of over-zealous spy-hunters. Also, I would warn fellow-tourists in North Wales of their danger of being held up by any Tom or Dick, and called upon in most un-British fashion to prove their innocence.

Yesterday I was quietly geologising on Halkyn Mountain, as I thought miles away from everybody. I was pounced upon by a crowd armed with sticks, with whom was a soldier. After being subjected to impertinent questions and offensive remarks, I was marched like a criminal to execution and was under arrest for hours, until released by a police sergeant who had been phoned for.

Yours truly,
Henry A. Rogers,
354 Westminster Road,
Liverpool.
April 30th 1915.

Anonymous letters to residents of Llangollen
The *Llangollen Advertiser* of Friday, 28 May 1915 published the following:

LORD BRYCE AND LLANGOLLEN ALIEN
A LETTER THAT DEMANDS RESPECT

Last week we printed a letter from Mr N. Weber, residing at Tywynfa, Llangollen. He was one of those who had received an anonymous letter signed, 'The Inhabitants of Llangollen', warning him to leave the town before nine o'clock on the night of the 12th inst. Mr Weber, a German by birth, has resided nearly all his life in England and is married to a Welsh lady. He is solo clarinet player of the Band of the Lothian and Border Horse Yeomanry, Edinburgh, and was a Sergeant of 3rd Lancashire Fusiliers at Bury for many years, having his conduct papers with 'good conduct'. Mrs Weber has just received the following letter from Lord Bryce, the House of Lords:

Dear Madam,

In reply to your letter, all I know is that the order for internments has gone out; but I should hope as I said in the debate in Parliament, that the War Office authorities released your husband after enquiry, and as he had good testimonials as to his character and career, those who were charged with his examination of aliens, would not direct him to be again interned, but to leave him to live in Llangollen with you. I was fully satisfied that he should be allowed his freedom and, if it would help you or him to send this letter to the authorities when he has to be examined. You or he may show it, and may say that I shall be willing to make a statement if desired on his behalf. Trusting that your wishes will not be disappointed.

Faithfully yours,
BRYCE.

The *Llangollen Advertiser* newspaper of Friday, 1 October 1915 contained this:

ARRESTED AS A SPY
LLANGOLLEN MAN'S REMARKABLE EXPERIENCE
DETAINED AT CARNARVON PENDING
ENQUIRIES

It is only two months since Llangollen was provided with a first-rate sensation by the arrest of Mr G. S. Griffith, of Castle Street, by the military authorities at Holyhead, who found him making notes in a pocket-book on the beach and regarding his behaviour as suspicious, brought him before the authorities for explanations which, of course, were readily forthcoming.

A second 'regrettable incident' at Holyhead is reported to have taken place on Wednesday, when another Llangollen man, Mr Tom K. Jervis, son of Mr Edward F. Jervis, Fish Dealer, Hall Street, Llangollen, was arrested there together with his assistant, and is still detained by the authorities at Carnarvon, pending the result of enquiries now being made at Llangollen.

Mr T. K. Jervis is in business as a peripatetic photographer. He moves from place to place taking outside views of business premises, groups of local celebrities and anything else that comes his way. He obtained the rudiments of his art at Llangollen, where he studied under Mr Martin, subsequently entering a studio at Wrexham. Three years or so ago he started on his own; and ever since he has been travelling the kingdom, for several months past operating in South Wales; and then making his way north-ward, through the Midlands, where he put in a good deal of time in the vicinity of his mother's home in the Worcester district, and so came to Bangor. At one time, he employed as many as three assistants on his tour, carrying quite a large amount of impediments; but business appears to have tapered off somewhat as he came north, and he reached Bangor with one assistant and a fine new outfit for snapshotting purposes. At Bangor good business was done, Mr Jervis taking quite the right course to put himself in order with the authorities by obtaining the necessary permission to continue his craft; and when all possible local orders had been met, he determined to pass on to the next most promising locality; and, unfortunately not profiting by Mr G. S. Griffith's experience, he decided that this should be Holyhead; and Holyhead it was.

With his assistant and cameras, he arrived at the station by rail on Wednesday morning; and, having his companion in charge of the artistic outfit, proceeded straight to the police station, to find out whether there was really any just cause or impediment why he should not get to work in the town, and whether he might not carry his camera through the streets as he had been permitted to do elsewhere.

From all accounts, he was told with official brevity and a degree of finality that warned him, it was no use appealing that he could do nothing of the kind. So, he hurried back to the railway station with the intent of retiring elsewhere if he found it impossible to place himself in order in Holyhead. Here he found his assistant and the camera had been taken into custody by the naval police; and; upon Mr Jervis disclosing his identity as the owner of the outfit, he was politely but firmly informed that he must 'come along too'. Needless to say, he went.

At the brief official examination at Holyhead, that followed as a matter of course, Mr Jervis was not able to establish his identity to the satisfaction of the authorities. He might claim to be 'Mr T. K. Jervis of Llangollen', but how did they know. Where was his ticket in connection with the 'National Registration Act', he was asked, and he could not produce it, it being in his father's keeping at Llangollen. Mr Griffith, it will be remembered, had little difficulty in this connection, quite a cloud of ministerial witnesses being prepared to vouch for his bona-fides. So, there was nothing to be done but to wire to Llangollen; and it was so.

Having wired to his father, telling with telegraphic conciseness, what had happened, the photographers were conveyed from Holyhead to Carnarvon; and here they were again interrogated. The authorities there appear to have been partly satisfied; at any rate, they granted them their liberty and permission to take up their abode at a temperance hotel where, presumably, they were kept under observation. As to their cameras and other incidentals, however, they comprised quite another story. The authorities were not going to relinquish their hold upon the outfit until they were thoroughly and completely satisfied, and without it Mr Jervis did not feel disposed to move; and perhaps it was just as well that he did not.

He wrote, however, to his father, at Llangollen, asking him to collect the data necessary to satisfy the authorities and without which he would remain under suspicion at Carnarvon. The data required included his birth certificate; a letter from his schoolmaster, minister and other responsible people; and, further, his identification card, under the 'National Registration Act'. Our representative left as Mr Edward F. Jervis was busily collecting these details; and needless to say, not a little perturbed by the mistake of the authorities. 'Why don't they catch Germans and not

Llangollen men', was his parting query; and to this he added, 'It won't take long to satisfy them all is right.' By the time these lines appear in print most possibly this has been done.

The Llangollen Museum located in Castle Street, Llangollen, has several photographs by 'Tommy Jervis' in its collection, some dating back to the 1920s. They are of Llangollen's streets and shops. It seems he was a quite prolific photographer – when he was not being detained by the authorities!

The 'Mr G. S. Griffith' referred to in the article was George Samuel Griffith, born at Llangollen in 1873. He resided at 41 Castle Street, Llangollen, and his occupation was that of a Calvinistic Methodist preacher, rather than German spy!

The *North Wales Weekly News* of Sunday, 3 October 1915 carried an advertisement prominently on its front page:

Startling Lecture by Mr. William Le Queux – The World Famous Author. Subject: 'German Spies and their Methods'.

Below it was a list of various towns in North Wales where over the following two weeks Mr William Le Queux would give his 'startling lecture'. Spy mania had taken off even before the start of the First World War, but now it was truly proceeding apace.

The Blackout!

When thinking of 'wartime blackouts' today, we immediately think of the Second World War. But such a thing existed in Britain, including North Wales, during the

First World War. This was done for two main reasons, the first being fear of Zeppelin raids, and the second fear of coastal attacks from enemy boats. The *North Wales Weekly News* of Thursday, 4 January 1917 carried its regular weekly timetable for the wartime blackout in North Wales for 4 January 1917 to 10 January 1917:

Date	Visible from sea	All other lights
January 4th	4.39	6.09
January 5th	4.41	6.11
January 6th	4.42	6.12
January 7th	4.43	6.13
January 8th	4.44	6.14
January 9th	4.46	6.16
January 10th	4.47	6.17

The times in the first column also apply to the lighting on lamps on vehicles including cycles.

A lighting offence

In the Thursday, 11 January 1917 edition of the *North Wales Weekly News*, this appeared:

Reverend Hugh Edwards, Frondirion, Old Colwyn, appeared before the Conway Sessions on Monday. Summoned for having an acetylene lamp on his motor cycle, the light of which had not been obscured. A technical offence admitted. He had put tissue paper over the glass as he returned from Beaumaris, but the light was so poor he had to remove it. On New Year's Day, he had an accident at Aber, near College Farm. P.C. Williams of Deganwy gave evidence that he had too bright a light. Reverend Edwards was fined 10 shillings by the Magistrates.

The blackouts and restrictions on vehicle lighting were not just implemented because of the risk of Zeppelin raids or the bombardment of coastal areas by German ships. There was fear and suspicion that night-signalling was taking place around the coastline of Britain by German spies or fifth-columnist British traitors. The police and military received thousands of generally well-intended reports of such illicit signalling during the course of the war, but the vast majority were false.

Further Reading

Dufeil, Yves. *Kaiserliche Marine U-Boote 1914-1918* (London: Hstomar Publications, 2011).

Fromm, Bella. *Blood and Banquets: A Berlin Social Diary* (US: Citadel Press, 2002).

Gerard, James W. *My Four Years in Germany* (United States: Robert J. Hall, 2015).

Hadley-McGill, Michael L. *Count Not the Dead: The Popular Image of the German Submarine* (Montreal: Queen's University Press, 1995).

Lewis-Stempel, John. *The War Behind the Wire – The Life, Death And Glory of British Prisoners of War, 1914 to 1918* (UK: Weidenfeld & Nickolson, 2014).

Olivia, M. T. *Daisy, Princess of Pless, by Herself* (London: John Murray, 1928).

Pirzio-Biroli, Corrado. *My Great-Grandfather, Grand-Admiral von Tirpitz – German Leader After Bismarck and Before Hitler* (Bloomington: Archway Publishing, 2016).

Sanders, Paul. *The British Channel Islands Under Occupation 1940-45* (Jersey: Jersey Heritage Trust, 2005).

Scheer, Reinhard (Admiral Scheer). *Germany's High Seas Fleet in the World War* (Truro: Shilka, 2013)

Von Langsdorff, Werner. *U-Boote am Feind* (Germany: C. Bertelsmann Gutersloh, 1937).

Von Tirpitz, Alfred Peter Friedrich. *My Memoirs by Grand Admiral Tirpitz: Volumes One and Two* (New York: Dodd, Mead and Company, 1919).

Acknowledgements

1. Thank you to my talented sister-in-law and friend, Sarah Jones of Denbigh, for her four fine contributions to this book, namely her sketch plan of Dyffryn Aled and its vicinity; her sketch of the Dyffryn Aled mansion; of the Dyffryn Aled sports field; and her depiction of the three German officer POWs signalling to the *U38* on the beach at Llandudno.

2. The National Archives, Kew, Richmond, Surrey.

3. The National Library of Wales/Llyfrgell Genedlaethol Cymru, Aberystwyth, Ceredigion.